William Shakespeare

THE TWO GENTLEMEN
OF VERONA

Edited with a Commentary by Norman Sanders
Introduced by Russell Jackson

PENGUIN BOOKS

PENGUIN BOOKS

Published by the Penguin Group
Penguin Books Ltd, 80 Strand, London WC2R ORL, England
Penguin Group (USA) Inc., 375 Hudson Street, New York, New York 10014, USA
Penguin Group (Canada), 90 Eglinton Avenue East, Suite 700, Toronto, Ontario, Canada M4P 2Y3
(a division of Pearson Penguin Canada Inc.)
Penguin Ireland, 25 St Stephen's Green, Dublin 2, Ireland (a division of Penguin Books Ltd)
Penguin Group (Australia), 250 Camberwell Road, Camberwell, Victoria 3124, Australia
(a division of Pearson Australia Group Pty Ltd)
Penguin Books India Pvt Ltd, 11 Community Centre, Panchsheel Park, New Delhi – 110 017, India
Penguin Group (NZ), cnr Airborne and Rosedale Roads, Albany, Auckland 1310, New Zealand
(a division of Pearson New Zealand Ltd)
Penguin Books (South Africa) (Pty) Ltd, 24 Sturdee Avenue, Rosebank 2196, South Africa

Penguin Books Ltd, Registered Offices: 80 Strand, London WC2R ORL, England

www.penguin.com

This edition first published in Penguin Books 1968
Reissued in the Penguin Shakespeare series 2005

This edition copyright © Penguin Books, 1968
Account of the Text and Commentary copyright © Norman Sanders, 1968
Further Reading copyright © Michael Taylor, 1997
General Introduction and Chronology copyright © Stanley Wells, 2005
Introduction, The Play in Performance and Further Reading copyright © Russell Jackson, 2005

Set in 11.5/12.5 PostScript Monotype Fournier
Designed by Boag Associates
Typeset by Palimpsest Book Production Limited, Polmont, Stirlingshire
Printed in England by Clays Ltd, St Ives plc

Contents

General Introduction

Every play by Shakespeare is unique. This is part of his greatness. A restless and indefatigable experimenter, he moved with a rare amalgamation of artistic integrity and dedicated professionalism from one kind of drama to another. Never shackled by convention, he offered his actors the alternation between serious and comic modes from play to play, and often also within the plays themselves, that the repertory system within which he worked demanded, and which provided an invaluable stimulus to his imagination. Introductions to individual works in this series attempt to define their individuality. But there are common factors that underpin Shakespeare's career.

Nothing in his heredity offers clues to the origins of his genius. His upbringing in Stratford-upon-Avon, where he was born in 1564, was unexceptional. His mother, born Mary Arden, came from a prosperous farming family. Her father chose her as his executor over her eight sisters and his four stepchildren when she was only in her late teens, which suggests that she was of more than average practical ability. Her husband John, a glover, apparently unable to write, was nevertheless a capable businessman and loyal townsfellow, who seems to have fallen on relatively hard times in later life. He would have been brought up as a Catholic, and may have retained

Catholic sympathies, but his son subscribed publicly to Anglicanism throughout his life.

The most important formative influence on Shakespeare was his school. As the son of an alderman who became bailiff (or mayor) in 1568, he had the right to attend the town's grammar school. Here he would have received an education grounded in classical rhetoric and oratory, studying authors such as Ovid, Cicero and Quintilian, and would have been required to read, speak, write and even think in Latin from his early years. This classical education permeates Shakespeare's work from the beginning to the end of his career. It is apparent in the self-conscious classicism of plays of the early 1590s such as the tragedy of *Titus Andronicus*, *The Comedy of Errors*, and the narrative poems *Venus and Adonis* (1592–3) and *The Rape of Lucrece* (1593–4), and is still evident in his latest plays, informing the dream visions of *Pericles* and *Cymbeline* and the masque in *The Tempest*, written between 1607 and 1611. It inflects his literary style throughout his career. In his earliest writings the verse, based on the ten-syllabled, five-beat iambic pentameter, is highly patterned. Rhetorical devices deriving from classical literature, such as alliteration and antithesis, extended similes and elaborate wordplay, abound. Often, as in *Love's Labour's Lost* and *A Midsummer Night's Dream*, he uses rhyming patterns associated with lyric poetry, each line self-contained in sense, the prose as well as the verse employing elaborate figures of speech. Writing at a time of linguistic ferment, Shakespeare frequently imports Latinisms into English, coining words such as abstemious, addiction, incarnadine and adjunct. He was also heavily influenced by the eloquent translations of the Bible in both the Bishops' and the Geneva versions. As his experience grows, his verse and prose become more supple,

the patterning less apparent, more ready to accommo-
date the rhythms of ordinary speech, more colloquial in
diction, as in the speeches of the Nurse in *Romeo and
Juliet*, the characterful prose of Falstaff and Hamlet's
soliloquies. The effect is of increasing psychological
realism, reaching its greatest heights in *Hamlet*, *Othello*,
King Lear, *Macbeth* and *Antony and Cleopatra*. Gradually
he discovered ways of adapting the regular beat of the
pentameter to make it an infinitely flexible instrument for
matching thought with feeling. Towards the end of his
career, in plays such as *The Winter's Tale*, *Cymbeline* and
The Tempest, he adopts a more highly mannered style,
in keeping with the more overtly symbolical and emblem-
atical mode in which he is writing.

So far as we know, Shakespeare lived in Stratford till
after his marriage to Anne Hathaway, eight years his
senior, in 1582. They had three children: a daughter,
Susanna, born in 1583 within six months of their marriage,
and twins, Hamnet and Judith, born in 1585. The next
seven years of Shakespeare's life are virtually a blank.
Theories that he may have been, for instance, a school-
master, or a lawyer, or a soldier, or a sailor, lack evidence
to support them. The first reference to him in print, in
Robert Greene's pamphlet *Greene's Groatsworth of Wit*
of 1592, parodies a line from *Henry VI, Part III*, implying
that Shakespeare was already an established playwright.
It seems likely that at some unknown point after the birth
of his twins he joined a theatre company and gained
experience as both actor and writer in the provinces and
London. The London theatres closed because of plague
in 1593 and 1594; and during these years, perhaps recog-
nizing the need for an alternative career, he wrote and
published the narrative poems *Venus and Adonis* and *The
Rape of Lucrece*. These are the only works we can be

certain that Shakespeare himself was responsible for putting into print. Each bears the author's dedication to Henry Wriothesley, Earl of Southampton (1573–1624), the second in warmer terms than the first. Southampton, younger than Shakespeare by ten years, is the only person to whom he personally dedicated works. The Earl may have been a close friend, perhaps even the beautiful and adored young man whom Shakespeare celebrates in his *Sonnets*.

The resumption of playing after the plague years saw the founding of the Lord Chamberlain's Men, a company to which Shakespeare was to belong for the rest of his career, as actor, shareholder and playwright. No other dramatist of the period had so stable a relationship with a single company. Shakespeare knew the actors for whom he was writing and the conditions in which they performed. The permanent company was made up of around twelve to fourteen players, but one actor often played more than one role in a play and additional actors were hired as needed. Led by the tragedian Richard Burbage (1568–1619) and, initially, the comic actor Will Kemp (d. 1603), they rapidly achieved a high reputation, and when King James I succeeded Queen Elizabeth I in 1603 they were renamed as the King's Men. All the women's parts were played by boys; there is no evidence that any female role was ever played by a male actor over the age of about eighteen. Shakespeare had enough confidence in his boys to write for them long and demanding roles such as Rosalind (who, like other heroines of the romantic comedies, is disguised as a boy for much of the action) in *As You Like It*, Lady Macbeth and Cleopatra. But there are far more fathers than mothers, sons than daughters, in his plays, few if any of which require more than the company's normal complement of three or four boys.

The company played primarily in London's public playhouses – there were almost none that we know of in the rest of the country – initially in the Theatre, built in Shoreditch in 1576, and from 1599 in the Globe, on Bankside. These were wooden, more or less circular structures, open to the air, with a thrust stage surmounted by a canopy and jutting into the area where spectators who paid one penny stood, and surrounded by galleries where it was possible to be seated on payment of an additional penny. Though properties such as cauldrons, stocks, artificial trees or beds could indicate locality, there was no representational scenery. Sound effects such as flourishes of trumpets, music both martial and amorous, and accompaniments to songs were provided by the company's musicians. Actors entered through doors in the back wall of the stage. Above it was a balconied area that could represent the walls of a town (as in *King John*), or a castle (as in *Richard II*), and indeed a balcony (as in *Romeo and Juliet*). In 1609 the company also acquired the use of the Blackfriars, a smaller, indoor theatre to which admission was more expensive, and which permitted the use of more spectacular stage effects such as the descent of Jupiter on an eagle in *Cymbeline* and of goddesses in *The Tempest*. And they would frequently perform before the court in royal residences and, on their regular tours into the provinces, in non-theatrical spaces such as inns, guildhalls and the great halls of country houses.

Early in his career Shakespeare may have worked in collaboration, perhaps with Thomas Nashe (1567–*c*. 1601) in *Henry VI, Part I* and with George Peele (1556–96) in *Titus Andronicus*. And towards the end he collaborated with George Wilkins (*fl.* 1604–8) in *Pericles*, and with his younger colleagues Thomas Middleton (1580–1627), in *Timon of Athens*, and John Fletcher (1579–1625), in *Henry*

VIII, *The Two Noble Kinsmen* and the lost play *Cardenio*.
Shakespeare's output dwindled in his last years, and he
died in 1616 in Stratford, where he owned a fine house,
New Place, and much land. His only son had died at the
age of eleven, in 1596, and his last descendant died in
1670. New Place was destroyed in the eighteenth century
but the other Stratford houses associated with his life are
maintained and displayed to the public by the Shakespeare
Birthplace Trust.

One of the most remarkable features of Shakespeare's
plays is their intellectual and emotional scope. They span
a great range from the lightest of comedies, such as *The
Two Gentlemen of Verona* and *The Comedy of Errors*, to the
profoundest of tragedies, such as *King Lear* and *Macbeth*.
He maintained an output of around two plays a year,
ringing the changes between comic and serious. All his
comedies have serious elements: Shylock, in *The Merchant
of Venice*, almost reaches tragic dimensions, and *Measure
for Measure* is profoundly serious in its examination of
moral problems. Equally, none of his tragedies is without
humour: Hamlet is as witty as any of his comic heroes,
Macbeth has its Porter, and *King Lear* its Fool. His greatest
comic character, Falstaff, inhabits the history plays and
Henry V ends with a marriage, while *Henry VI, Part III*,
Richard II and *Richard III* culminate in the tragic deaths
of their protagonists.

Although in performance Shakespeare's characters can
give the impression of a superabundant reality, he is not
a naturalistic dramatist. None of his plays is explicitly
set in his own time. The action of few of them (except
for the English histories) is set even partly in England
(exceptions are *The Merry Wives of Windsor* and the
Induction to *The Taming of the Shrew*). Italy is his
favoured location. Most of his principal story-lines derive

from printed writings; but the structuring and translation of these narratives into dramatic terms is Shakespeare's own, and he invents much additional material. Most of the plays contain elements of myth and legend, and many derive from ancient or more recent history or from romantic tales of ancient times and faraway places. All reflect his reading, often in close detail. Holinshed's *Chronicles* (1577, revised 1587), a great compendium of English, Scottish and Irish history, provided material for his English history plays. The *Lives of the Noble Grecians and Romans* by the Greek writer Plutarch, finely translated into English from the French by Sir Thomas North in 1579, provided much of the narrative material, and also a mass of verbal detail, for his plays about Roman history. Some plays are closely based on shorter individual works: *As You Like It*, for instance, on the novel *Rosalynde* (1590) by his near-contemporary Thomas Lodge (1558–1625), *The Winter's Tale* on *Pandosto* (1588) by his old rival Robert Greene (1558–92) and *Othello* on a story by the Italian Giraldi Cinthio (1504–73). And the language of his plays is permeated by the Bible, the Book of Common Prayer and the proverbial sayings of his day.

Shakespeare was popular with his contemporaries, but his commitment to the theatre and to the plays in performance is demonstrated by the fact that only about half of his plays appeared in print in his lifetime, in slim paperback volumes known as quartos, so called because they were made from printers' sheets folded twice to form four leaves (eight pages). None of them shows any sign that he was involved in their publication. For him, performance was the primary means of publication. The most frequently reprinted of his works were the non-dramatic poems – the erotic *Venus and Adonis* and the more moralistic *The Rape of Lucrece*. The *Sonnets*, which appeared in 1609, under his name but possibly without his consent, were less successful, perhaps because the vogue for sonnet sequences, which peaked in the 1590s, had passed by then. They were not reprinted until 1640, and then only in garbled form along with poems by other writers. Happily, in 1623, seven years after he died, his colleagues John Heminges (1556–1630) and Henry Condell (d. 1627) published his collected plays, including eighteen that had not previously appeared in print, in the first Folio, whose name derives from the fact that the printers' sheets were folded only once to produce two leaves (four pages). Some of the quarto editions are badly printed, and the fact that some plays exist in two, or even three, early versions creates problems for editors. These are discussed in the Account of the Text in each volume of this series.

Shakespeare's plays continued in the repertoire until the Puritans closed the theatres in 1642. When performances resumed after the Restoration of the monarchy in 1660 many of the plays were not to the taste of the times, especially because their mingling of genres and failure to meet the requirements of poetic justice offended against the dictates of neoclassicism. Some, such as *The Tempest* (changed by John Dryden and William Davenant in 1667 to suit contemporary taste), *King Lear* (to which Nahum Tate gave a happy ending in 1681) and *Richard III* (heavily adapted by Colley Cibber in 1700 as a vehicle for his own talents), were extensively rewritten; others fell into neglect. Slowly they regained their place in the repertoire, and they continued to be reprinted, but it was not until the great actor David Garrick (1717–79) organized a spectacular jubilee in Stratford in 1769 that Shakespeare began to be regarded as a transcendental genius. Garrick's idolatry prefigured the enthusiasm of critics such as Samuel Taylor Coleridge (1772–1834) and William Hazlitt (1778–1830). Gradually Shakespeare's reputation spread abroad, to Germany, America, France and to other European countries.

During the nineteenth century, though the plays were generally still performed in heavily adapted or abbreviated versions, a large body of scholarship and criticism began to amass. Partly as a result of a general swing in education away from the teaching of Greek and Roman texts and towards literature written in English, Shakespeare became the object of intensive study in schools and universities. In the theatre, important turning points were the work in England of two theatre directors, William Poel (1852–1934) and his disciple Harley Granville-Barker (1877–1946), who showed that the application of knowledge, some of it newly acquired, of early staging conditions to performance of the plays could render the original texts viable in terms of the modern theatre. During the twentieth century appreciation of Shakespeare's work, encouraged by the availability of audio, film and video versions of the plays, spread around the world to such an extent that he can now be claimed as a global author.

The influence of Shakespeare's works permeates the English language. Phrases from his plays and poems – 'a tower of strength', 'green-eyed jealousy', 'a foregone conclusion' – are on the lips of people who may never have read him. They have inspired composers of songs, orchestral music and operas; painters and sculptors; poets, novelists and film-makers. Allusions to him appear in pop songs, in advertisements and in television shows. Some of his characters – Romeo and Juliet, Falstaff, Shylock and Hamlet – have acquired mythic status. He is valued for his humanity, his psychological insight, his wit and humour, his lyricism, his mastery of language, his ability to excite, surprise, move and, in the widest sense of the word, entertain audiences. He is the greatest of poets, but he is essentially a dramatic poet. Though his plays have much to offer to readers, they exist fully only in performance. In these volumes we offer individual introductions, notes on language and on specific points of the text, suggestions for further reading and information about how each work has been edited. In addition we include accounts of the ways in which successive generations of interpreters and audiences have responded to challenges and rewards offered by the plays. The Penguin Shakespeare series aspires to remove obstacles to understanding and to make pleasurable the reading of the work of the man who has done more than most to make us understand what it is to be human.

Stanley Wells

The Chronology of Shakespeare's Works

A few of Shakespeare's writings can be fairly precisely dated. An allusion to the Earl of Essex in the chorus to Act V of *Henry V*, for instance, could only have been written in 1599. But for many of the plays we have only vague information, such as the date of publication, which may have occurred long after composition, the date of a performance, which may not have been the first, or a list in Francis Meres's book *Palladis Tamia*, published in 1598, which tells us only that the plays listed there must have been written by that year. The chronology of the early plays is particularly difficult to establish. Not everyone would agree that the first part of *Henry VI* was written after the third, for instance, or *Romeo and Juliet* before *A Midsummer Night's Dream*. The following table is based on the 'Canon and Chronology' section in *William Shakespeare: A Textual Companion*, by Stanley Wells and Gary Taylor, with John Jowett and William Montgomery (1987), where more detailed information and discussion may be found.

The Two Gentlemen of Verona	1590–91
The Taming of the Shrew	1590–91
Henry VI, Part II	1591
Henry VI, Part III	1591

Introduction

The Two Gentlemen of Verona, an engaging comedy of love, affords plenty of opportunities for witty repartee, elegant variations on familiar romantic themes and a considerable range of comic situations. It has one of Shakespeare's most memorable clowns – and his dog – and it deals with the conflict between love and friendship. It also takes its characters into darker areas of treachery and deceit, before arriving somewhat uncertainly at a resolution. In many respects it anticipates later plays by Shakespeare, partly because it shares with them the plot elements of romantic narrative: lovers and friends who are separated and brought back together in trying or dangerous circumstances; rings exchanged as tokens of love; a young woman disguising herself as a man; parents with absolute power to hinder the love-life of their children and then – in comedy at least – to relent. In the theatre the play has proved successful, especially in recent years, even though directors and actors have not always found ways of convincing audiences that the 'happy' ending has been earned by everyone, and that we can be confident that all the lovers, forgetting the wrongs that have been done (especially to the women), will be able to enjoy 'One feast, one house, one mutual happiness' (V.4.174).

FRIENDS AND LOVERS

The play begins amiably enough, with two young men debating the relative claims of the active and the reflective romantic life. Being young, well born, rich and Italian, they may be supposed to have a degree of sophistication and an easy command of the elegant language of love. One of them, Valentine, is off to travel, and wishes his friend was of the same mind. But Proteus is in love with a woman, and does not want to leave her behind, even to 'see the wonders of the world abroad' (I.i.6). From the very beginning the play approaches heterosexual love with a sense of its duality: it is both absurd and serious. Proteus's 'tender days' are chained to 'the sweet glances of [his] honoured love' (3–4), but he also speaks earnestly to Valentine as his loving friend:

> Wilt thou be gone? Sweet Valentine, adieu.
> Think on thy Proteus, when thou haply seest
> Some rare noteworthy object in thy travel.
> Wish me partaker in thy happiness,
> When thou dost meet good hap; and in thy danger –
> If ever danger do environ thee –
> Commend thy grievance to my holy prayers,
> For I will be thy beadsman, Valentine. (11–18)

In this he uses one simple, forceful religious metaphor. Proteus will pray for his friend as though he were a priest commissioned to do so – a 'beadsman' counting his rosary.

Proteus's plea to be remembered during his friend's travels is eloquent and direct, but he is answered with wordplay and satire. Proteus (says Valentine) is all set to be a 'lover', a comic character type with a predictable pattern of behaviour. It 'boots thee not', Valentine insists, 'To be in love, where scorn is bought with groans; | Coy looks, with heart-sore sighs' (I.1.29–30). The common-place attributes of the love-sick are rehearsed ('Yet writers say . . . And writers say . . .', 42, 45), together with a customary warning that 'by love the young and tender wit | Is turned to folly, blasting in the bud' (47–8). Valentine is voicing the conventional notion that lovers are transformed by their passion: in fact Proteus's name – that of a character in Homer's *Odyssey* who could change his shape at will – suggests that constancy is not going to be one of his strongest points. Valentine concludes, though, with a rueful, good-humoured and no less familiar acceptance that lovers are beyond persua-sion: 'But wherefore waste I time to counsel thee | That art a votary to fond desire?' (51–2). Left alone, Proteus reflects on the way his beloved Julia has 'metamorphosed' him (66), so that he remains moping at home, neglecting his studies, wasting his time and 'heart sick with thought' (69) while Valentine goes off in search of honour. For all the show of resistance he has put up to Valentine's arguments, he recognizes that he has 'Made wit with musing weak' (69).

Julia, as Proteus's beloved, begins by exhibiting the conventional waywardness of comic lovers. In the scene with her maid Lucetta (I.2) love makes her say one thing when she means another, changing moods and her mind unpredictably. Proverbial sayings are batted backward and forward like shuttlecocks between Julia and Lucetta – 'His little speaking shows his love but small. | Fire that's closest kept burns most of all' (29–30). In fact when Julia is alone the fuss she is making over Proteus's letter, desperate to read it but equally anxious not to seem concerned, provokes her to reflect on this far from unprecedented state of affairs. Not only is she governed by the proverbial tendency of 'maids' to say no 'in modesty' when they mean yes, but she knows she is behaving childishly – or rather, that 'Love' is: 'Fie, fie! How wayward is this foolish love, | That, like a testy babe, will scratch the nurse, | And presently, all humbled, kiss the rod.' (57–9). She calls Lucetta back, but still cannot bring herself to admit that she wants to know the letter's contents. It takes several minutes (encompassing seventeen lines of verse in which the two women pass musical metaphors back and forth) before she gets possession of the letter – only to tear it up in a frenzy of pretended indignation. Left alone again, Julia pieces the fragments together and lavishes her affection on them.

The scene, like many that will follow, is structured like a musical work, with a combination of duets and solos, and after what seems like Julia's concluding aria (I.2.104–29), a coda brings Lucetta back on stage to announce that dinner is waiting and Julia in a final flurry of pretended indifference leaves the pieces of paper to be collected by her maid. For all its mannered arrangement, though, the underlying suggestion is that strongly held feelings can't be hidden: Julia's extended, determined play with conventions of restraint is transparently disingenuous. Not so far underneath the surface is a language of dominance and discipline. The testy babe who first scratches the nurse then kisses the rod, 'all humbled', is love itself (or himself, Cupid) rather than the lover, but what is at stake is Julia's resistance or surrender to a superior power. The language of love is a topic the play returns to several times, often by way of eloquent and sustained efforts, like Valentine's poem (intercepted by the Duke of Milan in III.1.140–51), his soliloquy after he has been banished (III.1.170–87) and Proteus's advice to Thurio on wooing (III.2.68–70, 73–87).

However, the parting of Proteus and Julia (II.2.1–18) is no occasion for wordplay. Julia leaves 'without a word' to Proteus's surprise (though he has bid her 'Answer not' a couple of lines earlier) and he reflects that 'so true love should do; it cannot speak, | For truth hath better deeds than words to grace it.'

In Milan, the Duke's daughter Silvia plays out another cliché of courtship, that of the adored woman and her 'servants'. She enjoys the entertainment provided by her suitors' playing along with the convention and vying with each other for rank in her court. Valentine soon adapts to this way of life, and before long he and the suitor favoured by her father, Thurio, engage in a contest of wit in her presence, and she watches and listens approvingly: 'A fine volley of words, gentlemen, and quickly shot off' (II.4.32–3). This is one of the 'exercises' young men travel for, honing their skills of courtesy and eloquence by learning to pay court: the ability to be a conventionally witty lover is an accomplishment worth achieving. By a stroke of irony, it is his father's insistence on his acquiring some of these benefits that meanwhile propels Proteus away from Julia and provides the temptation to betray both her and Valentine. Without the experience of travel, Proteus 'cannot be a perfect man' (I.3.20). The advice of his father's servant Panthino neatly sums up the educational influence of a well-regulated court:

> There shall he practise tilts and tournaments,
> Hear sweet discourse, converse with noblemen,
> And be in eye of every exercise
> Worthy his youth and nobleness of birth. (30–33)

In these respects at least, becoming a 'perfect' man is within the grasp of any well-educated gentleman. By Valentine's account Proteus is already well on his way to this qualification, being 'complete in feature and in mind, | With all good grace to grace a gentleman' (II.4.71–2). Whether such accomplishments guarantee other kinds of perfection is another question, to which the play's events will lead.

So long as the contemplation of paradoxes is limited to the leisure pursuit of courting, the contradictions remain playful and hurt no one. Lovers are tortured by dilemmas that can be concisely expressed as irreconcilable opposites. They are blind, but have eyes for their mistress; they endure a kind of servitude, but it brings a kind of freedom; they never stop talking, but in fact are most eloquent when silent. Denied access to the object of their love, they tend to become melancholy. Julia recognizes the nature of passion in this way: 'The more thou dammest it up, the more it burns' (II.7.24). When separation is enforced in earnest, the effect is more severe. Valentine, banished from the court by Silvia's enraged father, laments that he has been effectively banished from himself: 'She is my essence, and I leave to be, | If I be not by her fair influence | Fostered, illumined, cherished, kept alive' (III.1.182–4). As it happens, he does not know that his plight is the consequence of a similar crisis in the personality of another lover.

Proteus's infatuation with Silvia has placed him in a dilemma that has no pleasure in it. In two soliloquies – separated by a short comic scene which allows him to go offstage and intensify his bewilderment in private – Proteus is suddenly a divided subject. The recurrent 'I' in the first speech (II.4.190–212) is part of a series of statements about his affections and actions: 'I love him not as I was wont . . . I love his lady . . . I love him so little . . . How shall I dote on her . . .', and so on. In Act II, scene 6, when he returns to the stage, he has recognized that the problematic 'I' denotes his very sense of his own selfhood:

> I cannot leave to love, and yet I do;
> But there I leave to love where I should love.
> Julia I lose, and Valentine I lose;
> If I keep them, I needs must lose myself;
> If I lose them, thus find I by their loss:
> For Valentine, myself; for Julia, Silvia.
> I to myself am dearer than a friend,
> For love is still most precious in itself . . . (17–24)

The notion that a person is 'dearer than a friend' to himself, stated as a self-evident truism, is the key to what rapidly develops into a career of breathtaking selfishness, even as Proteus pieces together the rationale for indulging his impulses at the expense of a friend and a lover. But the same way of speaking lends itself to convincing deception. Even after he has betrayed Valentine's plans to Silvia's father, Proteus can still speak the language of advice, with its glibly balanced statement of opposing considerations: 'Cease to lament for that thou canst not help, | And study help for that which thou lamentest' (III.1.241–2). Soon he will be bad-mouthing Valentine to Silvia (having volunteered to do this to clear the way for Thurio), tricking Thurio by arranging a serenade (in IV.2) for which he himself takes credit, giving Silvia the ring Julia gave him (unwittingly using the disguised Julia as a go-between) and, eventually, following Silvia into the forest and threatening to rape her when she refuses his advances. The only element of all this that cannot be laid to his account is the cruelty of employing Julia: everything else is done deliberately and in full knowledge of the likely outcome.

Although the idea of metamorphosis first appeared in the play's first scene (I.1.66) as a familiar and rueful reflection by Proteus on the effect of his love for Julia, it has now returned in a far more serious guise. When he reached the court of the Duke of Milan Valentine was turned into a lover – as Speed puts it, 'metamorphosed with a mistress' (II.1.28–9) – and Proteus, who was the pattern of a faithful and affectionate friend when the play opened, is now living up to his name as a shape-changer and has been transformed into a traitor. By contrast the women become exemplars of constancy. Julia, in particular, having embarked on a comic journey in male disguise in order to be with her lover, undergoes the torment of witnessing his suit to Silvia. To make matters worse, she is sent to Silvia with the ring she herself had given Proteus. Silvia is addressed in song as an example of virtues that neither Proteus nor Thurio possess: 'Holy, fair, and wise is she; | The heaven such grace did lend her, | That she might admirèd be' (IV.2.40–43). She refuses to let the 'subtle, perjured, false, disloyal man' off the hook, and only agrees to let him have her picture 'since [his] falsehood shall become [him] well | To worship shadows and adore false shapes' (126–7). As soon as she can, she makes her escape from the court, aided by Sir Eglamour, a 'gentleman' who seems the antitype of Proteus – not only is he 'Valiant, wise, remorseful, well-accomplished' (IV.3.13), but he is further qualified as faithful and virtuous by the vow of chastity he undertook when his 'true love' died. (In the event he also proves unreliable, but at this point in the play his virtues are the greatest thing about him.) Julia and Silvia may have been comically abject or imperious in their roles in the game of love, but as the play's plot grows less playful and more dangerous they prove to be courageous and resourceful when occasion demands.

LAW AND ORDER IN THE WOODS

The journey to the woods takes all the principal characters to a new place of learning as valuable in its own way as any court. The outlaws who capture Valentine are not high-principled exiles like the courtiers who follow the banished Duke in *As You Like It*: they have committed various passionate crimes, including at least one murder. Their new career of highway robbery is hardly contemplative or virtuous (although Valentine manages to extract goodness from the situation, as his short soliloquy at the beginning of V.4 indicates). At the same time they are examples (as one of their number explains) of the consequences of youthful passion: 'Know then that some of us are gentlemen, | Such as the fury of ungoverned youth | Thrust from the company of awful [that is, law-abiding] men.' (IV.1.44–6). The speaker left Verona after plotting to 'steal away a lady, | An heir, and near allied unto the Duke' (48–9), and one of his colleagues was banished from Mantua for stabbing another 'gentleman' in an impulsive moment ('in my mood', 50–51). They may not be exemplary asylum-seekers, but their account of themselves suggests the havoc that passion can wreak in men. Valentine's good looks, his claim to have killed a man and his accomplishments – in particular his skill in 'the tongues' – win him comically immediate election as their 'general', which he accepts once he has been

assured that they 'do no outrages | On silly [that is, inno-
cent] women or poor passengers' (71–2). This, and the
fact that one of the outlaws swears 'By the bare scalp of
Robin Hood's fat friar' (35), suggests at least a degree of
idealism. (It seems that the Nottinghamshire outlaw's
fame has reached Italy.) As brigands go they are
relatively harmless. Valentine may be stretching a point
when, in the play's closing moments, he solicits a free
pardon for them from the Duke on the grounds that,
'endued with worthy qualities', they are now 'reformèd,
civil, full of good, | And fit for great employment'
(V.4.154, 157–8). In performance, the audience may well
be too amused by their absurdity to take much notice of
this, but the outlaws do exemplify the process by which
men misled by passion can achieve a state deserving of
forgiveness.

In this they resemble Proteus, whose heinous crimes
against friendship and trust Valentine forgives after a
single, simple speech of penitence:

> My shame and guilt confounds me.
> Forgive me, Valentine; if hearty sorrow
> Be a sufficient ransom for offence,
> I tender't here; I do as truly suffer
> As e'er I did commit. (V.4.73–7)

Valentine's acceptance of this is even simpler, one of the
least complicated utterances in the play: 'Then I am paid'
(that is, satisfied). Sincere penitence is generously
accepted as full recompense for the wrongs done to him.
The appeal to Christian principles, explicit in what
follows, might in other circumstances be enough to
allay any scepticism in an audience's response: 'Who by
repentance is not satisfied | Is nor of heaven nor earth,

for these are pleased; | By penitence th'Eternal's wrath's appeased' (79–81). Mutual forgiveness and the religious precedents and precepts that hallow it are a recurring theme in Shakespeare's plays, including the comedic but wholly necessary reconciliations of *The Comedy of Errors* and the resonant plea for 'indulgence' by Prospero or the actor – or possibly even Shakespeare himself – in the closing lines of *The Tempest*. What follows here, however, propels the two gentlemen (and *The Two Gentlemen*) into an area of doubt and dismay. Valentine seals his generosity by giving Proteus 'All that was mine in Silvia' (83).

The immediate response to this comes from Julia, who swoons after exclaiming 'O me unhappy!' (I.4.84). Silvia says nothing, and after her reaction to Proteus's threat to rape her ('O heaven!') she remains silent for the remainder of the play. In the immediate aftermath of Valentine's offer it is Julia's business that is addressed. The ring she gave to Proteus, and which he ordered her to take to Silvia, is now identified, and with it, the 'page' herself. Again a simple speech focuses the moment of realization and shame for Proteus – 'How? Julia?' (101) – and she responds with a concise account of his treachery, an apology for her 'immodest' male disguise that is in fact an accusation, and a rhyming conclusion that puts a great deal of the business in a nutshell: 'It is the lesser blot, modesty finds, | Women to change their shapes than men their minds' – a thought that strikes home immediately with Proteus – 'Than men their minds? 'Tis true. O heaven, were man | But constant, he were perfect!' (109–12). It is Valentine who joins the hands of the couple, 'Let me be blest to make this happy close; | 'Twere pity two such friends should be long foes' (118–19). Both Julia and Proteus assent, agreeing that they have their 'wish for ever' (120), but Valentine's lines seem to invoke the friendship of the two men rather than love between the man and the woman. It is as though the focus has shifted back to the title characters.

Working out a balance sheet of who owes whom how much penitence is often begun in the final scene of a Shakespearian comedy, but rarely followed through. Not only is there no need to try the audience's patience with a prolonged session of plot summary and explanation, but the existence of loose ends may itself be a means of suggesting the similitude between the situations of a romantic fiction and the untidy experiences of 'real' life. This seems to be the prevalent effect in a number of the plays Shakespeare wrote some twenty years later. The ambitious onstage unravelling of a complex narrative in the final scene of *Cymbeline* (1610) marks that play out as an experiment in comic ethics and technique. (It even includes an offhand posthumous condemnation – Cymbeline's 'O, she was naught' (V.5.271) in reference to his dead queen – as well as some outstanding feats of forgiveness.) In other plays there is insufficient evidence in the script for the extent to which offended and offending characters are able to be utterly forgiving and sufficiently penitent. In *Measure for Measure* (1603) the Duke, who might be expected to be a source of wise justice, is himself an ambiguous and unconvincing do-gooder with a poor sense of other people's feelings. In the final scene of *All's Well That Ends Well* (1604–5) a callow and cruel young man responds to a staggeringly generous offer from the woman he has ill treated with brevity that seems not so much eloquently simple as heartlessly conditional. When Helena has explained the trick by which she fulfilled the conditions of bedding and ring-exchanging that secure her as his wife, Bertram assures the king that 'If she . . . can make me know this clearly', he will 'love her ever, ever dearly' (V.3.313–14). At least, though, some critics and audiences have found it possible to regard these uncertain 'comic' conclusions as daringly provocative. The problem with *The Two Gentlemen of Verona* lies in uncertainty as to the crafting of the final scene. In 1921 Sir Arthur Quiller-Couch, in his introduction to the Cambridge edition of the play, responded testily to 'All that is mine in Silvia I thee give' with the remark that 'one's impulse . . . is to remark that there are, by this time, *no* gentlemen in Verona'. Quiller-Couch is using 'gentlemen' in a characteristically Victorian and Edwardian sense, denouncing Valentine as a 'cad', but he has a point. Eight decades later, it is not only a desire for the play to work in terms of twenty-first-century feminist consciousness that prompts readers and audiences to wish that Silvia had at least been given some opportunity to express her feelings about the situation. In production she can, of course, be represented as too traumatized, and it can be suggested that Julia is also dismayed, but some gesture of inclusion or explanation might be expected in the play's text, even when a character does not speak for herself.

One explanation for the 'problem' of the ending may lie in the playwright's use of two principal sources, which differ markedly in their treatment of the same basic story. The tale of *Titus and Gisippus*, from Giovanni Boccaccio's collection of short fiction, the *Decameron* (1358), is concerned with a phenomenal example of the power of friendship. (As such it also figures in Sir Thomas Elyot's influential treatise on education and conduct, *The Book named the Governor*, published in 1531.) Gisippus is betrothed to a woman, but his friend Titus is dying – literally – for love of her; Gisippus gives up his claim to

her in order to save his friend's life. Later, in extreme
circumstances, Titus rescues Gisippus from abject poverty
and disgrace and betrothes him to his sister Fulvia.
'Friendship, then, is a sacred thing,' concludes the
narrator; 'She [friendship] deserves singular respect,
indeed she deserves to be commended with eternal praise,
for she is the most prudent of mothers, whose children
are generosity and propriety; her sisters are gratitude and
kindness; she is hostile to antipathy and greed, and is
always ready, without waiting to be asked, to do as she
would be done by.' The lesson is that 'only friendship'
can be relied on where other bonds – including those of
blood and marriage – fail.

Shakespeare's response to this declaration of faith may
be summed up in Proteus's bewildered, self-justifying
exclamation, 'In love, | Who respects friend?' (V.4.53–4),
and in the example of Valentine's generous response to
his wrongdoing.

The other principal source is an episode in Jorge de
Montemayor's *Diana* (1542). An English translation of
this Spanish romance was first published in 1598, but
Shakespeare may have known the story in the original,
from an unpublished translation or from a lost play, *The
History of Felix and Philiomena*, a performance of which
is known to have been given in 1595. In Montemayor's
romance a mysterious young woman, Felismena, having
saved a group of Portuguese shepherdesses from danger,
tells them how she was separated from her lover, Felix,
when his father sent him to a foreign court. She disguised
herself as a young man, taking the name Valerius, travel-
led to the court and was taken on as a page by Felix. He
employed her as a go-between in his wooing of a lady,
Celia, who unfortunately fell in love with the new envoy
and eventually died for unrequited love. Felix fled from

the court and now Felismena has followed him. At this
point the noise of a fight interrupts the story-telling, and
brings us back to the present situation: Felismena
discovers that Felix is nearby, warding off the attack of
three knights. With two well-aimed arrows she dispatches
two of the assailants, and Felix is able to deal with the
third. Felix, badly wounded, learns the identity of his
rescuer, who forgives him – but not before she has made
clear to him the consequences of his treachery. Felix
shows every sign of being about to die, but luckily is
revived so effectively that he begins 'to rekindle the old
love that he bore to Felismena', repents eloquently and
is forgiven by his victim. Here the prodigious generosity
is that of the wronged woman, who has transformed
herself in defiance of customary maidenly modesty into
a formidable fighter while her lover has degenerated
into treachery. In both the sources for the play the
respective emphases – on the extraordinary power of
friendship and the generosity of a strong and faithful
woman – are made clear within the narrative by the
characters' speeches and the narrator's voice. Shakespeare seems not to find appropriate ways of dramatizing
both divergent interpretations in his final scene. The
relationship between the two gentlemen takes centre
stage, and once the wrong done to Julia has been demonstrated and made good by penitence, the play hurries to
its close.

The men onstage do sort things out for themselves, of
course. The hapless Thurio arrives and tries to insist on
his right to Silvia, whom Valentine defends with the
appropriate male bravado:

Do not name Silvia thine; if once again,
Verona shall not hold thee. Here she stands;

Take but possession of her with a touch –
I dare thee but to breathe upon her love. (V.4.129–32)

Thurio replies with a degree of common sense ('I hold
him but a fool that will endanger | His body for a girl
that loves him not', 134–5), which to the Duke merely
demonstrates how 'degenerate and base' he is (137).
Consequently, the Duke offers Valentine, who is after all
'a gentleman, and well derived' (147), all that as a conventional patriarch is *his* (and would have been Thurio's) in
Silvia. What, exactly, is 'Silvia' then? In such transac-
tions, of course, all that is anyone's in Silvia includes a
great deal of money and an assured entry into the highest
levels of Milanese society. Women who play the role in
the twenty-first century may well feel that they have been
given a raw deal by Shakespeare, and that no amount of
scholarly knowledge of the marriage customs of the
play's time will help them cope with it. By now she has
been saved from rape by Valentine, surrendered by him
to the would-be rapist, laid claim to by a foolish suitor
and given by her father to Valentine. Even if we leave
aside several centuries of changed theatrical technique,
new notions of dramatic character and the ideas of (and
about) women in the role, can we confidently assume that
at some time in the play's career the final scene was satis-
fying? Did the Elizabethan audience contentedly watch
a boy-player in the role indicate the successive appropriate states of alarm and gratification, meanwhile
keeping out of the way of the speakers when Silvia was
not under discussion, until the moment came to form up
for a tableau of happiness? In the absence of any comment
from Shakespeare's own time, we have no way of
knowing how the play's ending was received.

Comparison with later plays may be helpful here. The

ending of *The Two Gentlemen of Verona* may have been poorly fashioned, but (as has been suggested already) an element of untidiness may even be thought to provide a useful element of realism, reflecting the untidiness of real life in such a way as to validate the overall effect of good humour and fortune. The most extreme example of this in Shakespeare's early work is the final act of *Love's Labour's Lost* (1594–5). There the Princess of France, suddenly informed of her father's death, sends away the King of Navarre and his courtiers. Their wooing, and the follies it has produced in them, have been welcome, but the men have too much to learn for a prematurely happy and marital ending to be possible. They must earn their happiness in a year and a day's exile in the real world of suffering and unhappiness. The self-consciousness of the drama is explicit: Berowne observes wryly that the period of exile is 'too long for a play' (V.2.867). *Twelfth Night* (1600–1601) ends with relative harmony, but Sebastian's loving friend Antonio is not provided for, and there is no guarantee that Malvolio will be successfully 'entreat[ed] to a peace' after his defiant and angry departure: 'I'll be revenged on the whole pack of you!' (V.1.377, 375). In *As You Like It* (1599–1600) Jaques insists on continuing to be an outsider and refuses to join in the 'rustic revelry' (V.4.174) that will celebrate the multiple weddings. In the final moments of *Much Ado About Nothing* (1598) Benedick proposes that Don John, the treacherous half-brother of Don Pedro, should be dealt with 'tomorrow', but the audience may remain unsure about young Claudio's credentials for marriage to a woman he has wronged – albeit mistakenly – and his reconciliation with his friend Benedick seems awkward. However, such gestures in the last moments of these plays are clearly marked, whereas in *The Two Gentlemen of Verona* the script as we have it seems unduly reticent just at the moment when an audience feels in need of more information on the feelings of two characters – and the fact that they are wronged women makes the situation especially worrisome.

THE SERVANTS' VIEW OF LIFE

To a considerable extent the play contains the sources for this scepticism, in the attitudes and experiences of a second group of characters – the servants. Silvia may enjoy treating her suitors as 'servants' (see II.1) but this charade depends on a strong sense of a social reality. Servants were a necessary part of the society in which the play was written, and men and women of 'gentle' condition would expect them to be on hand to do their fetching, carrying and message-bearing. In plays, though, servants have a valuable role, not merely as hired help but as performers with a double relationship to the audience and their fictional employers. Servants like the witty street-smart Speed and the sly but less voluble Launce exist to entertain the audience and – when appropriate – their masters. Sometimes comedy is generated by their failure to choose the right moment for this, a possibility that Shakespeare takes advantage of in *The Comedy of Errors* (1594), with its two sets of identical twins (servants and masters) providing multiple opportunities for confusion. The other dimension of the servants' performance is to offer a fresh view of their masters, either explicitly in comment on their doings or by the unconscious comparison and contrast. This is something the masters never seem to be aware of, so that in the *Two Gentlemen of Verona* Valentine and Proteus neither know nor care about the private life and opinions of Speed and Launce – who comes with his dog.

Julia's servant, Lucetta, is more fully in her employer's confidence than either of her male counterparts, and is a partner in the comedy of Julia's wooing by Proteus (I.2) and the pathos of the scene (II.7) in which she learns of his desertion of her and plans her secret departure from Verona and pursuit of him. However, Lucetta's role is not developed beyond this: she does not accompany her mistress to Milan. Even less substantial – though equally essential in the making of the play – Panthino advises Proteus's father Antonio to send his son away, and then is seen no more. It is Launce and Speed who carry the responsibility of looking askance at the behaviour of their social betters.

In the play's first scene the parting of the two friends is followed by some seventy lines (74–144) of comic cross-talk between Speed and Proteus, who has made the mistake of entrusting a letter for Julia to this unreliable messenger. The comic duologue corresponds at a lower social level to the wordplay between Valentine and Proteus, turning words and phrases back on themselves by punning and mistaking. Once he and his master have reached Milan (II.1) Speed offers a witty diagnosis of the 'special marks' (17) by which he can tell Valentine is in love. The catalogue characterizing the distracted lover is a conventional comic device that Shakespeare turned to later in *Much Ado About Nothing* (II.3), where Benedick bewails his friend Claudio's falling off from soldierly enthusiasms (such as an interest in armour) to sonnet-writing, and in *As You Like It* (III.2), where Rosalind as 'Ganymede' twits Orlando with not being enough of a lover.

At this point in *The Two Gentlemen of Verona* Speed's

solo turn serves to emphasize the metamorphosis that has overcome Valentine, and after eighty-eight lines of repartee unpacking such clichés as the blindness of Love and of lovers (II.1.60–73) he remains onstage to provide a sardonic commentary on the 'excellent motion' (puppet show, 89) between Silvia and her new suitor. Speed's last word (and having the last word matters a lot to a witty clown) reasserts a basic human need. Valentine may think he has 'dined' on Silvia's presence, but Speed knows better: 'Ay, but hearken, sir: though the chameleon Love can feed on the air, I am one that am nourished by my victuals, and would fain have meat. O, be not like your mistress; be moved, be moved' (163–6). It is Speed's wit, volubility and realism that immediately precede Proteus's parting from Julia, a parting that 'strikes poor lovers dumb' (II.2.20). When they leave the stage Launce and his dog, Crab, take possession of it.

Launce's account of his family's sorrow at the departure of their 'prodigious son' (II.3.3) is a comic tour de force, with its extravagant domestic details ('our cat wringing her hands', 7) and the suggestion that the subject is too formidable to be grappled with successfully. For all its comedy, this is a speech about the difficulty of expressing feelings. Launce needs an array of properties – hat, shoes, staff and dog – to try to convey the pathos of the scene. All the while, of course, 'the dog is himself' (21), intractably refusing to impersonate anyone, 'speak a word' (24) or simulate an emotion. Whenever either or both of the servants are onstage they offer, more or less consciously, a fresh perspective on the conduct of their masters. The short scene (II.5) that separates Proteus's two soliloquies on his sudden passion for Silvia focuses on the two subjects: Proteus's parting from Julia and Valentine's transformation into 'a notable lover' (37).

Launce accompanies Proteus onstage in Act III, Scene 1 and then remains to comment. Left alone, Launce reflects, 'I am but a fool, look you, and yet I have the wit to think my master is a kind of knave' (261), but rather than waste indignation on this he calmly proceeds to consider the pros and cons of his own love-life, and the prospects of marriage to a milkmaid who for all her faults 'hath more qualities than a water-spaniel' (269–70). Speed's arrival is the cue for a hundred lines of double-act on the topic, cut short only by Speed's announcement that Proteus is waiting for his servant.

As the end approaches, the two principal comic servants are removed. Speed accompanies Valentine to the forest, but after their first encounter with the outlaws no more is seen or heard of him. Launce's final performance, in Act IV, Scene 4, is the description of Crab's social gaffe in the Duke's house – making water under the dining table – and his own generosity in taking a whipping that would have punished the dog for his misbehaviour. The little fable of unselfish but unsentimental love ('When didst thou see me heave up my leg and make water against a gentlewoman's farthingale?', 35–6) is also a story of manners and status. Crab, an inappropriate substitute for the tiny pet Proteus intended for Silvia, had thrust himself 'into the company of three or four gentlemanlike dogs under the Duke's table' (16–17). Proteus's exasperated reaction to the fiasco is comic – 'didst thou offer her *this* from me?' (the emphasis actors usually prefer, 51) rarely fails to elicit a laugh – but his dismissal of his servant is harsh. After 'Away, I say! Stayest thou to vex me here?' (58) Launce leaves without a word, never to reappear. In terms of practicality the moment may be there to prompt Proteus's employment of the more gentlemanly 'Sebastian', whose 'face and . . . behaviour

. . . Witness good bringing up, fortune and truth' (64–6). Even so, his peremptory dismissal of Launce (and his dog) banishes an act the audience has come to value, and further darkens the play. The moment also initiates another development in the plot, in which disguise takes on a serious aspect.

LOVE AND DISGUISE

Much of the appeal of the comedy of love lies in the readiness with which intelligent, self-aware individuals find themselves falling into predictable patterns of behaviour, acting out the satirical descriptions of lovers' distraction, obsessive eloquence and absorption in the pursuit of their beloved. The move from role-playing to disguise is not difficult. In Act III, Scene 1 the Duke only has to pretend to Valentine that he himself is an unsuccessful suitor to elicit a great deal of worldly advice on the techniques of wooing. 'That man that hath a tongue,' says Valentine, 'is no man, | If with his tongue he cannot win a woman' (104–5). When the Duke asks for advice about gaining access to a woman who is being kept away from him, Valentine is easily led to suggest the very rope-ladder technique that he intends to adopt for Silvia's sake, and it is not long before the Duke, asking to try on Valentine's cloak (the recommended method of concealing such a ladder) uncovers the evidence. The scene runs through the conventions of wooing in a new way, but it also glances at the economics of wedding: the Duke wants to woo his own lady in order to cut off his daughter's inheritance, punishing her refusal of Thurio. The fictional lady's family (her 'friends') are keeping her locked up because they have promised her to 'a youthful gentleman of worth' (106–7), and Silvia's father in fact presents himself as a more mature equivalent of Valentine himself. Although the comic revelation of Valentine's ineptly concealed strategy is the main point of the scene, it reflects tellingly on the play's story. All the Duke needs to do is invoke another cliché of romance: he presents himself as a suitor trying to reach his beloved rather than the 'blocking parent' who tries in vain to keep young lovers apart in traditional comic plots.

The most complex disguise – although equally familiar as a romantic plot device – is Julia's impersonation of Sebastian. Like the 'saucy lackey' Ganymede, whom Rosalind impersonates in order to escape from her tyrannous uncle's court in *As You Like It*, Sebastian will be a 'well-reputed page' and a fashionable youth. Rather than cut her hair, Julia will 'knit it up in silken strings | With twenty odd-conceited true-love knots' (II.7.43–6). In Act IV, scene 4, when Julia knows the extent of her lover's betrayal, she turns the disguise inside out as she answers Silvia's sympathetic enquiries about the mistress Proteus has wronged. Asked how tall she was, Sebastian replies, 'About my stature.' However, the explanation goes further, taking Julia into a dimension of theatrical pathos:

> . . . for, at Pentecost,
> When all our pageants of delight were played,
> Our youth got me to play the woman's part
> And I was trimmed in Madam Julia's gown,
> Which servèd me as fit, by all men's judgements,
> As if the garment had been made for me; . . .
> And at that time I made her weep agood,
> For I did play a lamentable part.
> Madam, 'twas Ariadne passioning

For Theseus' perjury and unjust flight;
Which I so lively acted with my tears
That my poor mistress, movèd therewithal,
Wept bitterly; and would I might be dead
If I in thought felt not her very sorrow. (155–69)

Julia as Sebastian invents a story in which he, dressed as
Julia, performed the lamentation of a fictional abandoned
mistress (Ariadne), moving Julia (in the story) to tears
while (still in the story) experiencing her own sorrow 'in
thought' as an actor. In Shakespeare's time, with a young
man playing Julia, the effect would be further enhanced
by the appeal of the actor's own disguise as a woman
dressed as a fetching, fashionable young man. This vertig-
inous fiction, presenting two impersonations through the
assumed persona of another and adding to the piquancy
(with a greater or lesser homoerotic appeal) of the
theatre's use of cross-gender disguise, occurs at the point
in the plot of *The Two Gentlemen of Verona* where the
truth or falsity of a lover – in the sense of his proving
faithful or faithless – is about to be tested. Silvia herself,
unprotected by male disguise, is preparing for a hazardous
escape to the forest.

The Two Gentlemen of Verona is likely to be Shakespeare's earliest theatrical work. The first documented
reference to it, as *Gentlemen of Verona*, occurs in 1598 in
a list of Shakespeare's plays included by the clergyman
and literary enthusiast Francis Meres in his account of
England's literary achievements, *Palladis Tamia*. On
grounds of style and content, scholars have placed its
composition between the late 1580s and the mid 1590s.
The play was not published until the First Folio, in 1623,
and there is no record of performance until the eighteenth century. There are mistakes in the geography of

Italy – notably what seems to be a journey by water from Verona to Milan – and uncertainties in the naming of places. Such inconsistencies, together with others less easily remedied (of which a fuller account will be found in An Account of the Text), suggest that the Folio text represents an unrevised draft of the script. Whether such mistakes in themselves reflect the writer's lack of experience is debatable, but unsurprisingly it has been common to approach *The Two Gentlemen of Verona* as a dry run for Shakespeare's later comedies, a store-house of plot motifs and comic ideas that would later be incorporated in more mature and accomplished works. Some of these elements derive from the plays' common origins in the stock-in-trade of romantic fiction where disguises, separations, betrayals and (usually) some restoration of happiness abound. Julia's disguise and her commission as Sebastian anticipate Viola's situation in *Twelfth Night* where as 'Cesario' she is sent to woo Olivia on behalf of Count Orsino, whom she loves. Julia's situation, wooing on behalf of a treacherous lover with the very ring she had given him, is much more painful than Viola's, but male disguise, a ring and a confusion of emotions are common to both heroines. The outlaws, as has already been suggested, are not the exiled idealists of *As You Like It*, but Duke Senior's readiness in that play to find 'tongues in trees, books in the running brooks, | Sermons in stones, and good in everything' (II.1.16–17) has its counterpart in Valentine's appreciation of the 'shadowy desert, unfrequented woods' that give him undisturbed leisure and the 'complaining notes' of a nightingale to tune his 'distresses, and record [his] woes' (V.4.2, 5–6). Valentine, however, is preoccupied with keeping his lost love's image fresh in his memory: he is constant to the love that 'metamorphosed' him when he encountered Silvia. It is part of the play's compare-and-contrast method that no sooner has he uttered his desire to maintain faith as a lover than '*Noises within*' (12) herald the appearance onstage of the faithless Proteus. The dispatch of a young man to a court to acquire some polish anticipates Bertram's departure, first to the court and thence to the wars, in *All's Well That Ends Well*, and the confrontation of Proteus with the woman he has wronged – and the evidence of a ring – is echoed in the ending of the same play.

Other similarities with later comedies result from the adoption of features of popular theatre, such as the opportunities given to clowns for their verbal and visual comedy skills as performers in their own right. There is always the additional benefit of implicit or explicit comparison between the clowns' values and behaviour and those of their social superiors, and disguises adopted by enterprising young women give rise not only to comic confusion but emotional conflict and reflections on the wider topic of role-playing in life and love.

CHARACTERS AND CONVENTIONS

In some respects, anxieties about the play's effectiveness, and the extent to which it is convincing to modern audiences, can be answered by considering the limitations of the 'characters' in general. Elizabethan conventions of characterization differed from the psychological realism that has dominated European – and especially American – drama since the middle of the twentieth century. The lovers, both male and female, may be lent a degree of reality in performance by the audience's ability to accept the presence of a living actor as signifying a more complex and complete human being than is denoted by the role itself – the lines spoken and actions required by the script. In this case, the lovers exist by and through conventions of love, both comic and lyrical. They cannot go far beyond the limits of this discourse, lively and effective in execution to varying degrees. Their saving grace is a humorous self-consciousness that allows them to stand back and wonder at the way they find themselves speaking. Thus Valentine, having insisted that Proteus's beloved is fit only to 'bear his lady's train', justifies his 'braggardism' (II.4.157, 162) by insisting that she is the only possible object of his thought or regard. To Proteus's suggestion that he 'let her alone' he responds with,

> Not for the world! Why, man, she is mine own;
> And I as rich in having such a jewel
> As twenty seas, if all their sand were pearl,
> The water nectar, and the rocks pure gold. (166–9)

In Act II, Scene 2 Proteus recommends to Thurio a thoroughly conventional approach to lyricism, advising him to make more of an effort to persuade Silvia with what the Duke (agreeing) calls 'heaven-bred poesy':

> Say that upon the altar of her beauty
> You sacrifice your tears, your sighs, your heart;
> Write till your ink be dry, and with your tears
> Moist it again, and frame some feeling line
> That may discover such integrity;
> For Orpheus' lute was strung with poets' sinews,
> Whose golden touch could soften steel and stones,
> Make tigers tame, and huge leviathans
> Forsake unsounded deeps to dance on sands. (III.2.72–81)

Behaviour, like words, can follow tried and trusted formulas: Valentine outlines a scheme of wooing to the Duke in Act III, Scene 1, supporting his suggestions with such commonplace (and male) proverbial lore as 'A woman sometimes scorns what best contents her' (93).

The events of the play – particularly in the final scene – take the characters beyond such formulas of feeling, speech and action, but the characters do not find any adequate language for expressing the nature of their situation. Proteus's disorientation at the point (in II.4 and 6) where he realizes he must betray his friend and his mistress has already been quoted: it is expressed tellingly but formally, and there is none of the sense of expression pushed to its limits that marks the bewilderment of the anguished, divided men of plays written later in Shakespeare's career – Troilus, Hamlet, Angelo in *Measure for Measure* or Posthumus Leonatus in *Cymbeline*. *The Two Gentlemen of Verona* allows its clowns to comment by word and example on the behaviour of its elegant lovers, but it lacks the telling critique of conventional eloquence that in the more elaborated poetic world of *Love's Labour's Lost* prompts Berowne to insist that in times of real distress, 'Honest plain words best pierce the ear of grief' (V.2.748).

LOVE, SEX AND LANGUAGE

Not only does the play's account of the language of love fail to express these deeper divisions, but it also encompasses very little of the sensual, erotic dimension of human relationships. Although *The Two Gentlemen of Verona* deals with love, it does so with hardly any sense of the erotic. In this respect its imaginative world is

closer to that of John Lyly's stylish comedies of the 1580s
than Marlowe's *Hero and Leander* or Shakespeare's own
Ovidian narrative, *Venus and Adonis* (1592–3).
Shakespeare's Venus describes her own attractions in
terms apparently unknown to Valentine, Proteus, Julia
and Silvia:

> Thou canst not see one wrinkle in my brow;
> Mine eyes are grey and bright and quick in turning;
> My beauty as the spring doth yearly grow,
> My flesh is soft and plump, my marrow burning;
>   My smooth moist hand, were it with thy hand felt,
>   Would in thy palm dissolve or seem to melt. (139–44)

From the play's first scene the psychology of love is char-
acterized by means of witty comparisons and wordplay.
In Valentine's definition of the state of mind, every posi-
tive is countered by a negative in a logical reduction to
absurdity:

> To be in love, where scorn is bought with groans;
> Coy looks, with heart-sore sighs; one fading moment's
>   mirth,
> With twenty, watchful, weary, tedious nights;
> If haply won, perhaps a hapless gain;
> If lost, why then a grievous labour won;
> However, but a folly bought with wit,
> Or else a wit by folly vanquishèd. (I.1.29–35)

Great emphasis is placed on the illogical nature of the
passion, and images are introduced and developed to
provide apt illustrations – such as the 'sweetest bud' and
the 'eating canker' invoked by Valentine and countered
by Proteus in the same discussion (42–50). Ordered by

his father to follow his friend to Milan, Proteus reflects
on the fragility of his happiness in four well-turned
rhyming lines:

> O, how this spring of love resembleth
>   The uncertain glory of an April day,
> Which now shows all the beauty of the sun,
>   And by and by a cloud takes all away. (I.3.84–7)

Sensuous qualities are invoked to make comparisons more
vivid, by attributing feeling to the natural objects referred
to. Valentine, insisting on the supremacy of his beloved,
proclaims that she is his own, and he 'as rich in having
such a jewel | As twenty seas, if all their sand were pearl,
| The water nectar, and the rocks pure gold' (II.4.167–9).
Julia later compares her emotions with a stream that rather
than being 'dammed up' is allowed to flow evenly:

> . . . when his fair course is not hinderèd,
> He makes sweet music with th'enamelled stones,
> Giving a gentle kiss to every sedge
> He overtaketh in his pilgrimage. (II.7.27–30)

Bodily parts hardly figure at all in the lovers' discourse.
In Act III, Scene 1 Proteus promises that Valentine's
letters to Silvia will be delivered 'Even in the milk-white
bosom of [his] love' (250), but this is no more than a
conventional intimacy. The only occasion on which the
physical sensations of love are directly evoked is when
Julia, anxious to cherish the pieces of the letter she has
torn up, promises to 'kiss each several paper for amends'
(I.2.108). Finding the scrap with the words '*love-wounded
Proteus*' she promises, 'my bosom, as a bed, | Shall lodge
thee till thy wound be throughly healed; | And thus I

search it with a sovereign kiss' (113–16). The image of
the lover's name nestled in her bosom is more nurturing
than erotic, and the medical metaphor (she will 'search'
the wound like a surgeon) immediately supersedes it. The
effect is mild indeed, compared to Venus's urgent evocation of physical sensation.

This restraint may well have been more appropriate
in a publicly performed play than a privately enjoyed
erotic poem, but there is also very little bawdy humour,
even where one might expect it – among the servants.
Compared with such aggressive dealers in sexual wordplay as the two servants of the house of Montague who
begin the first brawl in *Romeo and Juliet*, Launce and
Speed are mild-mannered. In Act II, scene 5 Speed inter-
rogates Launce about Proteus and Julia – 'how stands
the matter with them?' – and is told: 'Marry thus: when
it stands well with him, it stands well with her' (19–21).
The actor only needs a few deft moves with Launce's
staff to make this plain enough, but the wordplay moves
swiftly on to the more innocent territory of 'understanding' and 'standing under', without developing the
bawdy potential of the idea. Similarly, Launce's account
of the woman he has admitted to falling in love with
(III.1.26 etc.) makes only the chastest of references to
physical intimacy: '*She is not to be kissed fasting, in respect
of her breath*' (315–16). In Act II, scene 7, when Julia is
discussing her disguise as a 'well-reputed page', the maid-
servant insists that she must have a codpiece, at which
her mistress protests: 'Out, out, Lucetta, that will be ill-
favoured.' Here the mild impropriety seems to be sub-
ordinated to satire at the expense of fashion: 'A round
hose, madam, now's not worth a pin, | Unless you have
a codpiece to stick pins on' (53–6). The disguise is
intended to protect its wearer from the 'loose encounters

of lascivious men' (41), but in the world of the play even the outlaws draw the line well short of such offences. (In the event, the only would-be rapist is the 'gentle' Proteus.)

Paradoxically, one effect of the comparative sexual innocence of *The Two Gentlemen of Verona* may be to liberate it: if the characters seemed more knowing, the way their fate is sorted out might seem even less acceptable. Moreover, this innocence does not preclude other kinds of sophistication. On one level, the play explores mutability – the metamorphoses of friends into lovers, the instability of the language of love, and the inconstancy that seems to be an unavoidable element of at least male humanity. It also exhibits the versatility and effectiveness of its own medium. In the scene (IV.2) where the disguised Julia witnesses Proteus's wooing of Silvia and (incidentally) his deception of Thurio, the accommodating host of the inn who has been brought along to enjoy what he takes to be the entertainment is surprised to discover that his young friend 'delight[s] not in music'. 'Hark what fine change is in the music!' he insists, meaning variation or modulation, but she responds, 'Ay; that change is the spite' referring to a change the host cannot perceive. To his question, 'You would have them play always one thing?', Silvia replies, 'I would always have one play one thing' – shifting 'play' away from its musical and into its theatrical meaning (64, 66–9). Shakespeare returned frequently to such scenes of overhearing where only the audience appreciates the full significance of what is going on, and which may have different meanings for the various characters onstage. It is not only the comic servants but the play's own theatricality that glances quizzically at the behaviour of lovers. In this respect at least *The Two Gentlemen of Verona*, for all its relative simplicity, and despite the apparent foreshortening of its concluding scene, is a sophisticated comedy.

Russell Jackson

The Play in Performance

'The devotion between two kids can take your breath away' – Adrian Hall, director of the 1994 production at the Delacorte Theatre in Central Park, New York, summed up in an interview one of the insights afforded by staging *The Two Gentlemen of Verona* in terms of contemporary youth culture (*Village Voice*, 16 August 1994). Shifting the play's period and locale has been the strategy of more than one successful production, and has also freed the play from a solemn duty to be representative of all that was best in its own culture. It has become an enjoyable, if at times perplexing, play about young people.

It is arguable that the relative frequency of the comedy in theatrical repertoires during the last thirty years, after centuries of relative neglect, has something to do with modern audiences' readiness to think of Shakespeare's plays in terms of their own society. We are so used to 'modern dress' in Shakespearian performances that we tend to forget that it has only been a familiar habit for a few decades. The most elaborate production of *The Two Gentlemen of Verona* in the nineteenth century – staged by Augustin Daly in New York and London in 1894–5 – garbled the play's plot in order to favour an elaborate 'Renaissance' setting, additional music and the principal

performer, Ada Rehan, who played Julia. Productions in
the early twentieth century were undistinguished and
half-hearted, and the Cambridge edition edited by John
Dover Wilson and Sir Arthur Quiller-Couch – whose
low opinion of the alleged 'gentlemen' has been quoted
above in the Introduction – does its best to clear
Shakespeare of responsibility by arguing for the dominant hand of an inept and anonymous reviser in the
play's less successful passages and its various minor
errors. A BBC radio version, broadcast in 1934, was frank
in its disregard for a play valued only for occasional lyrical
achievements and its fitful foreshadowing of better comedies to come: 'By declining to emphasize the ins and outs
of the plot [the adaptor, Barbara Burnham] has made
room for several more or less appropriate lyrics from
Herrick and others and for much contemporary Italian
music' (*The Times*, 15 January 1934). Reviewers tended
to respond in kind, praising directors for coping with
the play's perceived weaknesses, commiserating with the
need (at the Old Vic in particular) to 'complete' the performed canon – and simply wishing it were better.

No apologies were made by the New York Shakespeare
Festival, under Joseph Papp, which brought its characteristic energy and innovatory zeal to the play in 1957
with a Central Park production on a 'portable, collapsible,
truck-borne, four-angled stage with a multiplicity of
stairs and entrances and balconies' and a plethora of
eccentric stage business: dancing bears, striptease, a
weightlifter and more. In this frenetic context, performances were allowed an energy that more staid interpretations have missed: Anne Meara was 'a red-headed Julia
with a brash mingling of modesty and hoydenish vivacity'
(*New York Herald Tribune*, 23 July 1957). Other productions showing a Verona in the here-and-now have

included a 'pop' version directed at the Bristol Old Vic in 1967, with sets of twisted coloured plastic and music from a local pop group. The result was 'a swinging Shakespeare that should remove some of the academic carbuncles', according to the *Western Daily Press* (10 November 1967).

Two Gentlemen (without the '*The*'), first seen in Central Park in 1971, was effectively a new musical, with a book by John Guare and Mel Shapiro. It was in some respects a successor to *Hair*, which also had 'soft-rock' music by Galt MacDermot and celebrated the new-found liberation from social and political and, especially, moral restraint. *Variety* reported that it had discarded the theme of friendship to concentrate on 'how to see to it that boy gets girl after boy has met girl but girl comes burdened with some difficult problems' (11 August 1971). Even granting that 'friendship' might be sidelined, this was a ruthless simplification of the play, but the production was in any case determined to connect with modern issues (the Duke of Milan, rather than banishing Valentine, intended to have him drafted for the army). At the end, wrote Brendan Gill in the *New Yorker*, the audience longed to join in the celebration of 'the merry band of marvellous young people on stage who, notable for the variety of their sizes, shapes and hues, stood singing and dancing and blowing soap-bubbles and flaunting yo-yos and tossing Frisbees from box to box and hugging and kissing one another with the mingled joy and relief that people feel who have brought off something against heavy odds, something good and difficult' (11 December 1971).

Some other modern-dress versions have offered more quizzical, less determinedly happy interpretations. In 1970 at Stratford-upon-Avon, Robin Philips made Verona 'a high-class resort' and Milan 'an open-air university, with

the Duke as the avuncular Vice-Chancellor' (Peter
Thomson in *Shakespeare Survey* 24). The onstage swim-
ming pool and the atmosphere of moneyed leisure evoked
a 'gilded youth' among whom self-indulgent shifts of
affection and passion might be shrugged off. Helen Mirren
played Julia as an impatient teenager, maturing fast as
experience crowds in on her. Proteus (Ian Richardson),
physically less formidable than his glamorous friend, was
clearly out to compensate for his lack of athletic prowess.
The play opened with a silhouetted tableau of the principal characters: Patrick Stewart (Launce) entered and
walked slowly among them, fixing his social betters with
a sardonic gaze – a sombre figure, accompanied by a
black Labrador. Meanwhile the Beatles' 'All You Need is
Love' was heard, and the same effect was repeated at the
play's conclusion, punctuated by cuckoo-calls. This
created a very different effect from the 'love-in' of *Two
Gentlemen*. For all the amiable eccentricity of some scenes
and characters (notably Sebastian Shaw's idealistic scout-
master, Eglamour) the director made it clear that reality
lay elsewhere, ready to crush what one reviewer called
'a collection of worthless aristocratic layabouts without
even the depth of passion that renders Romeo's behaviour tolerable' (*Financial Times*, 24 July 1970). Edward
Hall's 1998 Royal Shakespeare Company production, also
set in modern Italy, had Julia progress from high heels
and a classy, short party frock, as the happy centre of
attention in Verona, to drab casual wear as a morose
teenage 'Sebastian', while Silvia, bright and brittle in her
happy state when she could tease her suitors, was shocked,
bewildered and bedraggled by the time she reached the
forest. Both productions offered a version of Italy that
encompassed high fashion and a stylish *dolce vita*, but the
second treated it less censoriously than the first.

(Consequently, in Hall's version the unavoidably comic-opera outlaws were less incongruous.) Paradoxically, Hall's was more sombre in its presentation of the events of the final scene.

One lesson to be derived from this – that 'modern dress' is by no means a simple category, but is capable of a wide range of inflections – can also be applied to other choices of period for the play. The 1970 Stratford production can hardly be said to have condoned the behaviour of its protagonists, even though Valentine signalled his forgiveness of Proteus by kissing him on the cheek he had earlier slapped in indignation at the news of Silvia's imprisonment. In 1957 at the Old Vic and 1968 in Regent's Park a 'late Romantic' setting served to account for the young men's extravagant behaviour. At the Old Vic Keith Michell played Proteus as a 'Byronic' hero – given to violent, self-serving emotional about-turns but at the same time dashing and irresistible. Confronted with his iniquity he placed a pistol to his temple – which prompted Valentine's offer of Silvia in an impulsive bid to prevent a tragic suicide. The set was 'a sort of ivy-clad Gothic folly, with fountains and blue woods melting in the distance' (*FT*, 23 January 1957). Less melodramatic, the 1968 open-air production in Regent's Park still allowed Peter Egan to 'suavely transform Proteus into a handsome Byronic cad' (*FT*, 18 July 1968). Nevertheless, in both versions the dominant effect was to reassure the audience that 'we are not, in fact, expected to believe very deeply in anything we see' (*FT*, 18 July 1968).

So-called 'traditional' costume and setting, whether evoking the Italian Renaissance or Shakespeare's own time, has proved no more uniform or predictable in its effect. Denis Carey's 1952 Bristol Old Vic production (also seen in London) sought to achieve a 'masque-like unreality' – in the words of the reviewer Ivor Brown it concealed the play's story 'in ribbons of grace and under a froth of humour'. A troupe of strolling *commedia dell'arte* players, 'touring Italy with false noses', interpolated songs by Julian Slade to round off scenes and keep up spirits. (In the final scene Valentine's offer of Silvia to Proteus was simply cut.) John Barton's two productions, both in double bills with other contemporary plays, located the comedy firmly in the theatrical conditions of Shakespeare's time. In both cases – for the Marlowe Society in Cambridge in 1951 (coupled with *Dr Faustus*) and for the RSC in Stratford-upon-Avon in 1981 (with *Titus Andronicus*) – the drastic cutting needed to fit the play into a somewhat rushed double-bill resulted in a sense of haste that removed subtleties and intensified difficulties of plot and characterization.

The choice of a setting in the 1920s or 1930s has brought other associations into play, usually with the support of appropriate popular music. A 1987 Regent's Park production evoked the world of P. G. Wodehouse – who after all described his novels as musical comedies without music – and for one reviewer it was only Proteus's catching the 'meaningful glint in Madeline Bassett's . . . sorry, Julia's eye' in the final scene that prevented him accepting Valentine's offer of Silvia (Simon Trussler, *Plays and Players*, October 1987). The evocation of Wodehouse's cooing but iron-willed ingénue, the bane of Bertie Wooster's life, helped to remove the edge from this far from promising moment. In David Thacker's popular 1991 RSC production – subsequently toured and given a West End revival – standards from the 1930s by Irving Berlin, Cole Porter and others framed the action. Between the scenes a female vocalist took the stage – accompanied by an onstage band

– with such numbers as 'More than you know, more than you know, | Man of my heart I love you so' and (for Act V) 'In the still of the night'. The resounding finale, sung by the entire cast, was 'That's the glory of love', which may have rounded matters off reassuringly, but also (as more than one critic noted) lent the play a kind of wry knowingness it didn't quite possess.

Reviewers, well versed in the pitfalls that threaten any company approaching the play, tend to announce the script's alleged inadequacies and then assess the extent to which they have been overcome. First-time audiences are more likely to accept what they see and hear (and perhaps wonder about it afterwards) and actors are on the whole inclined to take what chances they are offered. Proteus, for example, may be a 'problem' but he can also be an opportunity. Raul Julia and Carl Thomas made the title characters in *Two Gentlemen* 'terrific studs: they sing, dance and zap the audience with rare masculinity' (*Newsweek*, 11 December 1971). The 1994 New York production extended this sense of liberation into empowerment in more up-to-date terms: Julia sped off in pursuit of her lover riding pillion on the leather-clad Lucetta's Harley-Davidson. (Here come Thelma and Louise?) Barry Lynch, in David Thacker's 1991–2 RSC production, brought a saturnine slyness and insecurity to Proteus, while Richard Bonneville played Valentine 'as such a decent-hearted silly ass that his ludicrous offer is just the sort of fatuous thing you can imagine him blurting out in a moment of stress' (*Daily Telegraph*, 16 October 1992). The same production featured a memorable Thurio from Guy Henry, and also allowed the women room to develop their roles. In the London revival Josette Bushell-Mingo (who played Lucetta at Stratford) achieved 'a kind of gravity, elegance and nobility that naturally startle

Proteus and make him forget Julia', while Clare Holman as the wronged party was 'rather like a young Judi Dench, the voice half-hoarse, half-creamy, the manner so vital and spontaneous' (*FT*, 16 October 1992).

It is the servants though – in particular Launce – who have enjoyed most opportunities. In Peter Hall's fussy and self-consciously romantic 'Renaissance' production at Stratford in 1960 – the first play staged by the newly formed RSC and opening a season designed to explore the development of Shakespeare's comedies – Patrick Wymark was formidably earthy, with the true comedian's gift for playing off the audience's attention. John Russell Brown describes how Wymark 'animated his repetitive speeches by a variety of timing and emphasis, and based all on a sympathetic understanding of the large-minded, stubborn character who is yet at the mercy of circumstance' (*Shakespeare Survey* 14, 1961). Richard Moore, in the 1991–2 RSC production, illustrated the description of his departure from home by 'laying out his shoes, his socks and his arguments like fish on a slab' (Michael Coveney, *Observer*, 21 April 1991). Comedians from the variety stage and television have sometimes been cast in the part, with varying results. Jay Laurier, a favourite performer in Christmas pantomime, played Launce in his 'Idle Jack' make-up (permanently raised eyebrows and upturned nose) in an otherwise pallid production at Stratford-upon-Avon in 1938; Bernard Bresslaw, famous for his assumption of gormlessness in television comedy, appeared in Regent's Park in 1968, speaking (and singing) a good deal more than was set down for him; and Frankie Howerd, incomparably and lugubriously offended by life, was heard but alas not seen in a BBC radio broadcast in 1958.

At least on radio, though, the actor playing Launce is

unlikely to be upstaged by the dog playing Crab. Egged on by theatre publicity departments, newspapers (if not reviewers) and audiences have tended to make much of any animal appearing in this role. Aspersions on the play have often been accompanied by praise for the performer of Crab. Headlines such as 'Mongrel is star at Stratford' (*News Chronicle*, 21 April 1938) and 'Poor Play and a Good Dog' (*Birmingham Mail*, 6 April 1960) have not been uncommon. Woolly, who appeared in Thacker's production, acquired his own fan club, and Mark Hadfield, a Launce touchingly resigned to life's indignities, in the 1998 Stratford production, observed wistfully that inter- viewers seemed more anxious to learn about Cassie's offstage personality than his own work as an actor. It is after all in connection with the Elizabethan company manager Philip Henslowe's recipe for successful comedy – 'love – and a dog' – that *The Two Gentlemen of Verona* figures in *Shakespeare in Love*. The film does however suggest that the young playwright might do better: we see Will Kemp, as Launce, being upstaged by his dog, and Queen Elizabeth nods off during one of Valentine's speeches. This serves the film's purpose, but its life onstage in the last few decades suggests that the play can achieve an energy and appeal that this fictional version of Shakespeare's employer may not have reckoned with.

Russell Jackson

Further Reading

Like so much commentary on *The Two Gentlemen of Verona*, the two major editions of the play, Clifford Leech's Arden (1969) and Kurt Schlueter's New Cambridge (1990), do their best to make the play's gaucherie understandable (if not palatable) to the modern reader. While conceding that this early work is no masterpiece, Leech thinks it does have 'careful, and within its limits, subtle dramaturgy'. (In an earlier work by him, *Twelfth Night and Shakespearian Comedy* (1965), that control is seen as satiric.) Leech compares it to *All's Well That Ends Well*, *Pericles* and *Cymbeline*: they are all wandering plays, plays that change their locality more than once, as does the romance. It is indeed in terms of romance, or an early version of it, that Schlueter's New Cambridge edition defends the play, arguing that what is deemed ridiculous by many critics was intended to be ridiculous, and that, Cervantes-like, there is an intended and successful mixture of romance and satire (a frequent combination in romance). To see how well it works, Schlueter argues, we should discuss the play in relation to its sources, which he goes on to do. The greater part of his introduction, however, is taken up with an account of the play's history on the stage – perhaps a strategic retreat in the face of the text's infelicities. For a witty and pungent assault on these, the reader should consult H. B. Charlton's *Shakespearian Comedy* (1938).

Schlueter is not the first to see the play as a sophisticated departure from what has gone before. A. C. Hamilton's *The Early Shakespeare* (1967) argues that, despite the claims made for Lyly, *The Two Gentlemen of Verona* is the first real romantic comedy; and it is the first of Shakespeare's plays to handle a moral problem. He has no truck with the argument of the majority of critics that the moral problem is, to say the least, ineptly handled in what Robert Ornstein in *Shakespeare's Comedies* (1986) calls 'an unaccountably silly final scene', a final scene that E. M. W. Tillyard's *Shakespeare's Early Comedies* (1965) describes as 'morally and dramatically monstrous'. In contrast to the earlier, mainly Italian, versions of the tale, Hamilton says, Valentine's forgiveness of Proteus is admirably multifaceted: 'Proteus' repentance and Valentine's forgiveness and generosity astonish us as being both admirable and absurd, both ideal and simply human' – and this is what Shakespeare intended. E. C. Pettet's *Shakespeare and the Romance Tradition* (1949) makes equally large claims for the play's significance: 'it furnishes an almost complete anthology of the doctrine of romantic love . . . while its narrative, wholly concentrated on a serious love story, is pure romance'. For a balanced account of Shakespeare's debt to Lyly, G. K. Hunter's *John Lyly: The Humanist as Courtier* (1962) should be consulted, and so too should Leo Salingar's *Shakespeare and the Traditions of Comedy* (1974) and E. W. Talbert's *Elizabethan Drama and Shakespeare's Early Plays* (1963).

If one way to defend and explain the play is backward, through an examination of its sources, another is forward to Shakespeare's later and more successful

romantic comedies. Many critics take this route, deeming
The Two Gentlemen of Verona to be a tyro's preliminary
handling of the tricky theatrical and literary conventions
of romantic love. J. A. Bryant Jr's _Shakespeare and the
Uses of Comedy_ (1986) takes this position as does Stanley
Wells's 'The Failure of _The Two Gentlemen of Verona_',
in _Shakespeare Jahrbuch_ 94 (1963). Although she thinks
it a feeble play, Muriel Bradbrook in _Shakespeare and
Elizabethan Poetry: A Study of his Earlier Work in Relation
to the Poetry of his Time_ (1951) also stresses its importance in Shakespeare's development of romantic comedy:
the theme of the fashioning of the courtier leads to _A
Midsummer Night's Dream_. Bertrand Evans, in the course
of an investigation of the play's structure in _Shakespeare's
Comedies_ (1960), also thinks the play important for what
comes later but replaces _Dream_ with _Twelfth Night_ as its
mature development. And, taking Hamilton's line, Evans
finds Shakespeare's much reviled treatment of Proteus
typically, not to say gloriously, Shakespearian: 'Not only
cannot villainy harm innocence, it is even prevented from
doing irreparable harm to itself.'

Some defences of _The Two Gentlemen of Verona_ are
perhaps more glorious than sensible. John Arthos in
Shakespeare: The Early Writings (1972) sees in the play
the defeat of Neoplatonism by the problems of evil. R.
G. Hunter's _Shakespeare and the Comedy of Forgiveness_
(1965) thinks the final scene celebrates a _Christian_ forgiveness on Valentine's part in response to Proteus's contri-
tion. W. W. Lawrence's _Shakespeare's Problem Comedies_
(1931) believes that an Elizabethan audience would accept
the last scene on the basis of the huge cultural value of
friendship. W. T. MacCary's _Friends and Lovers: The
Phenomenology of Desire in Shakespearean Comedy_ (1985)
takes a similar line. The most abstract defence can be

found in John Vyvyan's *Shakespeare and the Rose of Love: A Study of the Early Plays in Relation to the Medieval Philosophy of Love* (1960) which sees the play almost entirely in the benumbing terms of Neoplatonic allegory.

Even if the final scene is (finally) indefensible, the most rewarding criticism of the play as a whole (and perhaps also of the final scene) is that which responds to its uncertain attempts to combine satire with romance and romantic comedy. That is, it's important to see why Launce and Speed (and Crab) – forebears of the likes of Sir Toby Belch and Touchstone – are in the same play as Julia, Valentine, Proteus and Silvia. As Schlueter notes, the first group are there to 'parody all kinds of misplaced idealisms in the world of this play'. Alexander Leggatt's *Shakespeare's Comedy of Love* (1974) responds to the play's heterogeneity, noting, among other things, the almost choric function of the satiric mirroring of the clowns, and the importance, generally speaking, of the outside world breaking in on the closed world of the lovers. Even that infamous final scene can be partially salvaged if seen in the larger social terms that the play may be advocating, as in Camille W. Slights's book, *Shakespeare's Comic Commonwealth* (1993), which defends the final scene as being 'less evocative of what it feels like to fall in love than a comic exploration of the nature and function of a gentleman'. *The Two Gentlemen of Verona*, as Leggatt says, may not be easy to like, but, as he also says, it has a quality of its own, 'cool, reticent and somewhat rueful, counselling us, if it counsels anything, not to expect too much'. Of the courtly world, that is, but also perhaps of itself.

Michael Taylor, 1997

The New Arden (3rd series) edition, edited by William C. Carroll (2004), includes valuable discussion of the issues of friendship in the play and its sources, and makes copious reference to the play in performance. In the edition by Paul Werstine and Barbara Mowat for the New Folger Library (1999), Jeffrey Masten's essay '*The Two Gentlemen of Verona*: A Modern Perspective' considers the ways in which Renaissance definitions of same-sex love are at work in the play. On this dimension of the play in its own time see also Bruce Smith's 'Making a Difference: Male/Male "Desire" in Tragedy, Comedy and Tragi-comedy', in *Erotic Politics*, edited by Susan Zimmerman (1992), and J. L. Simmons's 'Coming Out in Shakespeare's *The Two Gentlemen of Verona*', *ELH* 60 (1993). Michael Shapiro's *Gender in Play on the Shakespearean Stage: Boy Heroines and Female Pages* (1994) is a comprehensive and perceptive general study of cross-gender disguise; a sprightly and brief account will be found in Barbara Hodgdon's essay, 'Sexual Disguise and the Theatre of Gender', in *The Cambridge Companion to Shakespearean Comedy*, edited by Alexander Leggatt (2001). In '*The World Must be Peopled*': *Shakespeare's Comedies of Forgiveness* (2002) Michael D. Friedman proposes ways of approaching this and other plays that will reconcile feminist goals with the texts' apparent desire to achieve forgiveness for men at the expense of wronged women. The play's use of its source materials and its relationship with other plays figure in Leah Scragg's *Shakespeare's Mouldy Tales: Recurrent Plot Motifs in Shakespearean Drama* (1992) and its performance history is surveyed by Carol Jones Carlisle and Patty Derrick in a contribution to *Shakespeare's Sweet Thunder: Essays on the Early Comedies*, edited by Michael J. Collins (1997). Two useful anthologies of critical essays can also be recommended: Pamela Mason's *Shakespeare: Early Comedies* in the Casebook series (1995) and June Schlueter's *'The Two Gentlemen of Verona': Critical Essays* (1996). Finally, Crab makes an appearance in an article by Matthew Bliss, 'Property or Performer? Animals on the Elizabethan Stage', *Theatre Studies* 39 (1991), alongside such less tractable rivals as the hungry and homicidal bear in *The Winter's Tale*.

Russell Jackson, 2005

THE TWO GENTLEMEN
OF VERONA

The Characters in the Play

The DUKE of Milan
SILVIA, his daughter and the beloved of Valentine
THURIO, a foolish suitor for Silvia's hand
EGLAMOUR, Silvia's accomplice in her flight from Milan
PROTEUS ⎫
VALENTINE ⎬ the two gentlemen of Verona
JULIA, the beloved of Proteus, later disguised as
    Sebastian, a page
ANTONIO, father of Proteus
LUCETTA, waiting-woman of Julia
SPEED, servant of Valentine
LAUNCE, servant of Proteus
PANTHINO, servant of Antonio
HOST of the Inn where Julia lodges in Milan
OUTLAWS, led by Valentine during his banishment
SERVANT
Musicians
Attendants
Crab, a dog

Enter Valentine and Proteus

VALENTINE

Cease to persuade, my loving Proteus;
Home-keeping youth have ever homely wits.
Weren't not affection chains thy tender days
To the sweet glances of thy honoured love,
I rather would entreat thy company
To see the wonders of the world abroad
Than, living dully sluggardized at home,
Wear out thy youth with shapeless idleness.
But, since thou lovest, love still, and thrive therein,
Even as I would when I to love begin.   10

PROTEUS

Wilt thou be gone? Sweet Valentine, adieu.
Think on thy Proteus, when thou haply seest
Some rare noteworthy object in thy travel.
Wish me partaker in thy happiness,
When thou dost meet good hap; and in thy danger –
If ever danger do environ thee –
Commend thy grievance to my holy prayers,
For I will be thy beadsman, Valentine.

VALENTINE

And on a love-book pray for my success?

PROTEUS

20 Upon some book I love I'll pray for thee.

VALENTINE

That's on some shallow story of deep love,
How young Leander crossed the Hellespont.

PROTEUS

That's a deep story of a deeper love,
For he was more than over-shoes in love.

VALENTINE

'Tis true; for you are over-boots in love,
And yet you never swam the Hellespont.

PROTEUS

Over the boots? Nay, give me not the boots.

VALENTINE

No, I will not; for it boots thee not.

PROTEUS   What?

VALENTINE

To be in love, where scorn is bought with groans;
30 Coy looks, with heart-sore sighs; one fading moment's
    mirth,
With twenty, watchful, weary, tedious nights;
If haply won, perhaps a hapless gain;
If lost, why then a grievous labour won;
However, but a folly bought with wit,
Or else a wit by folly vanquishèd.

PROTEUS

So, by your circumstance, you call me fool?

VALENTINE

So, by your circumstance, I fear you'll prove.

PROTEUS

'Tis Love you cavil at; I am not Love.

VALENTINE

Love is your master, for he masters you;
40 And he that is so yokèd by a fool,

Methinks should not be chronicled for wise.

PROTEUS

Yet writers say, as in the sweetest bud
The eating canker dwells, so eating love
Inhabits in the finest wits of all.

VALENTINE

And writers say, as the most forward bud
Is eaten by the canker ere it blow,
Even so by love the young and tender wit
Is turned to folly, blasting in the bud,
Losing his verdure even in the prime,
And all the fair effects of future hopes.   50
But wherefore waste I time to counsel thee
That art a votary to fond desire?
Once more adieu. My father at the road
Expects my coming, there to see me shipped.

PROTEUS

And thither will I bring thee, Valentine.

VALENTINE

Sweet Proteus, no; now let us take our leave.
To Milan let me hear from thee by letters
Of thy success in love, and what news else
Betideth here in absence of thy friend;
And I likewise will visit thee with mine.   60

PROTEUS

All happiness bechance to thee in Milan.

VALENTINE

As much to you at home. And so farewell.   *Exit*

PROTEUS

He after honour hunts, I after love.
He leaves his friends to dignify them more;
I leave myself, my friends, and all for love.
Thou, Julia, thou hast metamorphosed me,
Made me neglect my studies, lose my time,

War with good counsel, set the world at naught;
Made wit with musing weak, heart sick with thought.
   Enter Speed

SPEED
70   Sir Proteus, save you! Saw you my master?

PROTEUS
But now he parted hence to embark for Milan.

SPEED
Twenty to one then he is shipped already,
And I have played the sheep in losing him.

PROTEUS
Indeed, a sheep doth very often stray,
An if the shepherd be a while away.

SPEED You conclude that my master is a shepherd then,
and I a sheep?

PROTEUS I do.

SPEED Why then, my horns are his horns, whether I wake
80   or sleep.

PROTEUS A silly answer, and fitting well a sheep.

SPEED This proves me still a sheep.

PROTEUS True; and thy master a shepherd.

SPEED Nay, that I can deny by a circumstance.

PROTEUS It shall go hard but I'll prove it by another.

SPEED The shepherd seeks the sheep, and not the sheep
the shepherd; but I seek my master, and my master
seeks not me. Therefore I am no sheep.

PROTEUS The sheep for fodder follow the shepherd; the
90   shepherd for food follows not the sheep. Thou for
wages followest thy master, thy master for wages follows
not thee. Therefore thou art a sheep.

SPEED Such another proof will make me cry, 'baa'.

PROTEUS But dost thou hear? Gavest thou my letter to
Julia?

SPEED Ay, sir. I, a lost mutton, gave your letter to her,

a laced mutton; and she, a laced mutton, gave me, a
lost mutton, nothing for my labour.

PROTEUS Here's too small a pasture for such store of
muttons.   100

SPEED If the ground be overcharged, you were best stick
her.

PROTEUS Nay, in that you are astray; 'twere best pound
you.

SPEED Nay, sir, less than a pound shall serve me for
carrying your letter.

PROTEUS You mistake; I mean the pound – a pinfold.

SPEED

From a pound to a pin? Fold it over and over,
'Tis threefold too little for carrying a letter to your lover.

PROTEUS But what said she?   110

Speed nods

A nod?

SPEED Ay.

PROTEUS Nod-ay? Why, that's noddy.

SPEED You mistook, sir. I say she did nod; and you ask
me if she did nod, and I say 'Ay'.

PROTEUS And that set together is 'noddy'.

SPEED Now you have taken the pains to set it together,
take it for your pains.

PROTEUS No, no; you shall have it for bearing the letter.

SPEED Well, I perceive I must be fain to bear with you.   120

PROTEUS Why, sir, how do you bear with me?

SPEED Marry, sir, the letter very orderly, having nothing
but the word 'noddy' for my pains.

PROTEUS Beshrew me, but you have a quick wit.

SPEED And yet it cannot overtake your slow purse.

PROTEUS Come, come, open the matter in brief; what
said she?

SPEED Open your purse, that the money and the matter
    may be both at once delivered.

130 PROTEUS Well, sir, here is for your pains.

    He gives Speed money
    What said she?

SPEED Truly, sir, I think you'll hardly win her.

PROTEUS Why? Couldst thou perceive so much from her?

SPEED Sir, I could perceive nothing at all from her; no,
    not so much as a ducat for delivering your letter; and
    being so hard to me that brought your mind, I fear she'll
    prove as hard to you in telling your mind. Give her no
    token but stones, for she's as hard as steel.

140 PROTEUS What said she? Nothing?

SPEED No, not so much as 'Take this for thy pains'. To
    testify your bounty, I thank you, you have testerned me;
    in requital whereof, henceforth carry your letters your-
    self. And so, sir, I'll commend you to my master.

                                                      Exit

PROTEUS

    Go, go, be gone, to save your ship from wreck,
    Which cannot perish, having thee aboard,
    Being destined to a drier death on shore.
    I must go send some better messenger.
    I fear my Julia would not deign my lines,
150 Receiving them from such a worthless post.   *Exit*

I.2   *Enter Julia and Lucetta*

JULIA

    But say, Lucetta, now we are alone,
    Wouldst thou then counsel me to fall in love?

LUCETTA

    Ay, madam, so you stumble not unheedfully.

JULIA

    Of all the fair resort of gentlemen

    That every day with parle encounter me,

    In thy opinion which is worthiest love?

LUCETTA

    Please you repeat their names, I'll show my mind

    According to my shallow simple skill.

JULIA

    What thinkest thou of the fair Sir Eglamour?

LUCETTA

    As of a knight well-spoken, neat, and fine;   10

    But, were I you, he never should be mine.

JULIA

    What thinkest thou of the rich Mercatio?

LUCETTA

    Well of his wealth; but of himself, so so.

JULIA

    What thinkest thou of the gentle Proteus?

LUCETTA

    Lord, lord, to see what folly reigns in us!

JULIA

    How now, what means this passion at his name?

LUCETTA

    Pardon, dear madam; 'tis a passing shame

    That I, unworthy body as I am,

    Should censure thus on lovely gentlemen.

JULIA

    Why not on Proteus, as of all the rest?   20

LUCETTA

    Then thus: of many good, I think him best.

JULIA

    Your reason?

LUCETTA

    I have no other but a woman's reason:

I think him so, because I think him so.

JULIA
And wouldst thou have me cast my love on him?

LUCETTA
Ay, if you thought your love not cast away.

JULIA
Why, he, of all the rest, hath never moved me. *approached*

LUCETTA
Yet he, of all the rest, I think best loves ye.

JULIA
His little speaking shows his love but small.

LUCETTA
30   Fire that's closest kept burns most of all.

JULIA
They do not love that do not show their love.

LUCETTA
O, they love least that let men know their love.

JULIA
I would I knew his mind.

LUCETTA
Peruse this paper, madam.

JULIA (*reads*)
    To Julia. – Say, from whom?

LUCETTA
That the contents will show.

JULIA
Say, say, who gave it thee?

LUCETTA
Sir Valentine's page; and sent, I think, from Proteus.
He would have given it you; but I, being in the way,
40   Did in your name receive it; pardon the fault, I pray.

JULIA
Now, by my modesty, a goodly broker!

Dare you presume to harbour wanton lines?
To whisper and conspire against my youth?
Now, trust me, 'tis an office of great worth,
And you an officer fit for the place.
There take the paper. See it be returned,
Or else return no more into my sight.

LUCETTA

To plead for love deserves more fee than hate.

JULIA

Will ye be gone?

LUCETTA   That you may ruminate.   *Exit*

JULIA

And yet I would I had o'erlooked the letter.   50
It were a shame to call her back again,
And pray her to a fault for which I chid her.
What 'fool is she, that knows I am a maid,
And would not force the letter to my view,
Since maids, in modesty, say no to that
Which they would have the profferer construe ay.
Fie, fie! How wayward is this foolish love,
That, like a testy babe, will scratch the nurse,
And presently, all humbled, kiss the rod.
How churlishly I chid Lucetta hence,   60
When willingly I would have had her here.
How angerly I taught my brow to frown,
When inward joy enforced my heart to smile.
My penance is to call Lucetta back
And ask remission for my folly past.
What ho! Lucetta!

     Enter Lucetta

LUCETTA   What would your ladyship?

JULIA

Is't near dinner-time?

LUCETTA   I would it were,
    That you might kill your stomach on your meat,
    And not upon your maid.
        She drops and picks up the letter

JULIA
70 What is't that you took up so gingerly?

LUCETTA
    Nothing.

JULIA
    Why didst thou stoop then?

LUCETTA
    To take a paper up that I let fall.

JULIA
    And is that paper nothing?

LUCETTA
    Nothing concerning me.

JULIA
    Then let it lie for those that it concerns.

LUCETTA
    Madam, it will not lie where it concerns,
    Unless it have a false interpreter.

JULIA
    Some love of yours hath writ to you in rhyme.

LUCETTA
80 That I might sing it, madam, to a tune.
    Give me a note; your ladyship can set.

JULIA
    As little by such toys as may be possible.
    Best sing it to the tune of 'Light o'love'.

LUCETTA
    It is too heavy for so light a tune.

JULIA
    Heavy? Belike it hath some burden then?

LUCETTA

Ay, and melodious were it, would you sing it.

JULIA

And why not you?

LUCETTA   I cannot reach so high.

JULIA

Let's see your song. How now, minion!
        Julia snatches at the letter which Lucetta retains

LUCETTA

Keep tune there still, so you will sing it out;
And yet methinks I do not like this tune.   90
        Julia seizes the letter

JULIA

You do not?

LUCETTA   No, madam; it is too sharp.

JULIA

You, minion, are too saucy.

LUCETTA

Nay, now you are too flat;
And mar the concord with too harsh a descant.
There wanteth but a mean to fill your song.

JULIA

The mean is drowned with your unruly bass.

LUCETTA

Indeed, I bid the bass for Proteus.

JULIA

This babble shall not henceforth trouble me.
Here is a coil with protestation.
        She tears the letter
Go, get you gone, and let the papers lie.   100
You would be fingering them, to anger me.

LUCETTA (*aside*)

She makes it strange, but she would be best pleased
To be so angered with another letter.   *Exit*

JULIA
    Nay, would I were so angered with the same!
    O, hateful hands, to tear such loving words.
    Injurious wasps, to feed on such sweet honey,
    And kill the bees that yield it with your stings.
    I'll kiss each several paper for amends.
    Look, here is writ, *kind Julia*. Unkind Julia,
110   As in revenge of thy ingratitude,
    I throw thy name against the bruising stones,
    Trampling contemptuously on thy disdain.
    And here is writ, *love-wounded Proteus*.
    Poor wounded name, my bosom, as a bed,
    Shall lodge thee till thy wound be throughly healed;
    And thus I search it with a sovereign kiss.
    But twice or thrice was Proteus written down.
    Be calm, good wind, blow not a word away
    Till I have found each letter in the letter,
120   Except mine own name. That some whirlwind bear
    Unto a ragged, fearful, hanging rock,
    And throw it thence into the raging sea.
    Lo, here in one line is his name twice writ:
    Poor, forlorn Proteus, passionate Proteus,
    To the sweet Julia. That I'll tear away;
    And yet I will not, sith so prettily
    He couples it to his complaining names.
    Thus will I fold them one upon another.
    Now kiss, embrace, contend, do what you will.
      Enter Lucetta

LUCETTA
130   Madam,
    Dinner is ready, and your father stays.

JULIA
    Well, let us go.

LUCETTA

What, shall these papers lie like tell-tales here?

JULIA

If you respect them, best to take them up.

LUCETTA

Nay, I was taken up for laying them down.
Yet here they shall not lie for catching cold.
She picks up the pieces of the letter

JULIA

I see you have a month's mind to them.

LUCETTA

Ay, madam, you may say what sights you see;
I see things too, although you judge I wink.

JULIA

Come, come, will't please you go?   *Exeunt*   140

Enter Antonio and Panthino   I.3

ANTONIO

Tell me, Panthino, what sad talk was that
Wherewith my brother held you in the cloister?

PANTHINO

'Twas of his nephew Proteus, your son.

ANTONIO

Why, what of him?

PANTHINO   He wondered that your lordship
Would suffer him to spend his youth at home,
While other men, of slender reputation,
Put forth their sons to seek preferment out:
Some to the wars to try their fortune there;
Some to discover islands far away;
Some to the studious universities.   10
For any or for all these exercises

He said that Proteus your son was meet,
And did request me to importune you
To let him spend his time no more at home,
Which would be great impeachment to his age,
In having known no travel in his youth.

ANTONIO

Nor needest thou much importune me to that
Whereon this month I have been hammering.
I have considered well his loss of time,
And how he cannot be a perfect man,
Not being tried and tutored in the world.
Experience is by industry achieved,
And perfected by the swift course of time.
Then tell me, whither were I best to send him?

PANTHINO

I think your lordship is not ignorant
How his companion, youthful Valentine,
Attends the Emperor in his royal court.

ANTONIO

I know it well.

PANTHINO

'Twere good, I think, your lordship sent him thither.
There shall he practise tilts and tournaments,
Hear sweet discourse, converse with noblemen,
And be in eye of every exercise
Worthy his youth and nobleness of birth.

ANTONIO

I like thy counsel; well hast thou advised;
And that thou mayst perceive how well I like it,
The execution of it shall make known.
Even with the speediest expedition
I will dispatch him to the Emperor's court.

PANTHINO

Tomorrow, may it please you, Don Alphonso
With other gentlemen of good esteem   40
Are journeying to salute the Emperor,
And to commend their service to his will.

ANTONIO

Good company; with them shall Proteus go.
   Enter Proteus, reading a letter
And in good time; now will we break with him.

PROTEUS (*aside*)

Sweet love, sweet lines, sweet life!
Here is her hand, the agent of her heart;
Here is her oath for love, her honour's pawn.
O, that our fathers would applaud our loves,
To seal our happiness with their consents!
O heavenly Julia!   50

ANTONIO

How now? What letter are you reading there?

PROTEUS

May't please your lordship, 'tis a word or two
Of commendations sent from Valentine,
Delivered by a friend that came from him.

ANTONIO

Lend me the letter. Let me see what news.

PROTEUS

There is no news, my lord, but that he writes
How happily he lives, how well beloved,
And daily gracèd by the Emperor;
Wishing me with him, partner of his fortune.

ANTONIO

And how stand you affected to his wish?   60

PROTEUS

As one relying on your lordship's will,
And not depending on his friendly wish.

ANTONIO

    My will is something sorted with his wish.
    Muse not that I thus suddenly proceed;
    For what I will, I will, and there an end.
    I am resolved that thou shalt spend some time
    With Valentinus in the Emperor's court.
    What maintenance he from his friends receives,
    Like exhibition thou shalt have from me.
70   Tomorrow be in readiness to go.
    Excuse it not, for I am peremptory.

PROTEUS

    My lord, I cannot be so soon provided.
    Please you deliberate a day or two.

ANTONIO

    Look what thou wantest shall be sent after thee.
    No more of stay; tomorrow thou must go.
    Come on, Panthino; you shall be employed
    To hasten on his expedition.

                          Exeunt Antonio and Panthino

PROTEUS

    Thus have I shunned the fire for fear of burning,
    And drenched me in the sea, where I am drowned.
80   I feared to show my father Julia's letter,
    Lest he should take exceptions to my love,
    And with the vantage of mine own excuse
    Hath he excepted most against my love.
    O, how this spring of love resembleth
        The uncertain glory of an April day,
    Which now shows all the beauty of the sun,
        And by and by a cloud takes all away.
    Enter Panthino

PANTHINO

    Sir Proteus, your father calls for you.
    He is in haste; therefore, I pray you go.

PROTEUS

> Why, this it is; my heart accords thereto,   90
> And yet a thousand times it answers, 'No.' *Exeunt*

*

Enter Valentine and Speed   II.1

SPEED

> Sir, your glove.

VALENTINE   Not mine. My gloves are on.

SPEED

> Why then, this may be yours, for this is but one.

VALENTINE

> Ha! Let me see. Ay, give it me, it's mine.
> Sweet ornament that decks a thing divine.
> Ah, Silvia, Silvia!

SPEED Madam Silvia! Madam Silvia!

VALENTINE How now, sirrah?

SPEED She is not within hearing, sir.

VALENTINE Why, sir, who bade you call her?

SPEED Your worship, sir, or else I mistook.   10

VALENTINE Well, you'll still be too forward.

SPEED And yet I was last chidden for being too slow.

VALENTINE Go to, sir. Tell me, do you know Madam
Silvia?

SPEED She that your worship loves?

VALENTINE Why, how know you that I am in love?

SPEED Marry, by these special marks: first, you have
learned, like Sir Proteus, to wreathe your arms, like a
malcontent; to relish a love-song, like a robin-redbreast;
to walk alone, like one that had the pestilence; to sigh,   20
like a schoolboy that had lost his A B C; to weep, like a
young wench that had buried her grandam; to fast, like

one that takes diet; to watch, like one that fears robbing;
to speak puling, like a beggar at Hallowmas. You were
wont, when you laughed, to crow like a cock; when you
walked, to walk like one of the lions; when you fasted,
it was presently after dinner; when you looked sadly, it
was for want of money. And now you are metamorphosed with a mistress, that, when I look on you, I can
hardly think you my master.

VALENTINE Are all these things perceived in me?

SPEED They are all perceived without ye.

VALENTINE Without me? They cannot.

SPEED Without you? Nay, that's certain; for without you
were so simple, none else would. But you are so without
these follies, that these follies are within you, and shine
through you like the water in an urinal, that not an eye
that sees you but is a physician to comment on your
malady.

VALENTINE But tell me, dost thou know my lady Silvia?

SPEED She that you gaze on so, as she sits at supper?

VALENTINE Hast thou observed that? Even she I mean.

SPEED Why, sir, I know her not.

VALENTINE Dost thou know her by my gazing on her,
and yet knowest her not?

SPEED Is she not hard-favoured, sir?

VALENTINE Not so fair, boy, as well-favoured.

SPEED Sir, I know that well enough.

VALENTINE What dost thou know?

SPEED That she is not so fair as, of you, well favoured.

VALENTINE I mean that her beauty is exquisite, but her
favour infinite.

SPEED That's because the one is painted, and the other
out of all count.

VALENTINE How painted? And how out of count?

SPEED Marry, sir, so painted to make her fair, that no
man counts of her beauty.

VALENTINE How esteemest thou me? I account of her beauty.

SPEED You never saw her since she was deformed.   60

VALENTINE How long hath she been deformed?

SPEED Ever since you loved her.

VALENTINE I have loved her ever since I saw her, and still I see her beautiful.

SPEED If you love her, you cannot see her.

VALENTINE Why?

SPEED Because Love is blind. O, that you had mine eyes, or your own eyes had the lights they were wont to have, when you chid at Sir Proteus for going ungartered!

VALENTINE What should I see then?   70

SPEED Your own present folly, and her passing deformity; for he, being in love, could not see to garter his hose; and you, being in love, cannot see to put on your hose.

VALENTINE Belike, boy, then you are in love; for last morning you could not see to wipe my shoes.

SPEED True, sir; I was in love with my bed. I thank you, you swinged me for my love, which makes me the bolder to chide you for yours.

VALENTINE In conclusion, I stand affected to her.

SPEED I would you were set, so your affection would   80
cease.

VALENTINE Last night she enjoined me to write some lines to one she loves.

SPEED And have you?

VALENTINE I have.

SPEED Are they not lamely writ?

VALENTINE No, boy, but as well as I can do them. Peace, here she comes.

       Enter Silvia

SPEED (*aside*) O excellent motion! O exceeding puppet! Now will he interpret to her.   90

VALENTINE Madam and mistress, a thousand good morrows.

SPEED (*aside*) O, give ye good even! Here's a million of manners.

SILVIA Sir Valentine and servant, to you two thousand.

SPEED (*aside*) He should give her interest, and she gives it him.

VALENTINE

As you enjoined me, I have writ your letter
Unto the secret nameless friend of yours;
Which I was much unwilling to proceed in,
But for my duty to your ladyship.

He gives her the letter

SILVIA I thank you, gentle servant, 'tis very clerkly done.

VALENTINE

Now trust me, madam, it came hardly off;
For, being ignorant to whom it goes,
I writ at random, very doubtfully.

SILVIA

Perchance you think too much of so much pains?

VALENTINE

No, madam; so it stead you, I will write,
Please you command, a thousand times as much;
And yet —

SILVIA

A pretty period! Well, I guess the sequel;
And yet I will not name it; and yet I care not;
And yet take this again;

She offers him the letter

                        and yet I thank you,
Meaning henceforth to trouble you no more.

SPEED (*aside*)

And yet you will; and yet, another 'yet'.

VALENTINE
 What means your ladyship? Do you not like it?
SILVIA
 Yes, yes; the lines are very quaintly writ;
 But, since unwillingly, take them again.
 Nay, take them.
  She offers the letter again
VALENTINE   Madam, they are for you.
SILVIA
 Ay, ay; you writ them, sir, at my request,
 But I will none of them; they are for you.   120
 I would have had them writ more movingly.
  Valentine takes the letter
VALENTINE
 Please you, I'll write your ladyship another.
SILVIA
 And when it's writ, for my sake read it over;
 And if it please you, so; if not, why, so.
VALENTINE
 If it please me, madam, what then?
SILVIA
 Why, if it please you, take it for your labour.
 And so, good morrow, servant.   *Exit*
SPEED (*aside*)
 O jest unseen, inscrutable, invisible
 As a nose on a man's face, or a weathercock on a steeple!
  My master sues to her; and she hath taught her suitor,   130
  He being her pupil, to become her tutor.
  O excellent device! Was there ever heard a better,
  That my master, being scribe, to himself should write
      the letter?
VALENTINE How now, sir? What are you reasoning with
 yourself?

SPEED Nay, I was rhyming; 'tis you that have the reason.

VALENTINE To do what?

SPEED To be a spokesman from Madam Silvia.

VALENTINE To whom?

140 SPEED To yourself. Why, she woos you by a figure.

VALENTINE What figure?

SPEED By a letter, I should say.

VALENTINE Why, she hath not writ to me.

SPEED What need she, when she hath made you write to yourself? Why, do you not perceive the jest?

VALENTINE No, believe me.

SPEED No believing you, indeed, sir. But did you perceive her earnest?

VALENTINE She gave me none, except an angry word.

150 SPEED Why, she hath given you a letter.

VALENTINE That's the letter I writ to her friend.

SPEED And that letter hath she delivered, and there an end.

VALENTINE I would it were no worse.

SPEED I'll warrant you, 'tis as well:

For often have you writ to her; and she, in modesty,
Or else for want of idle time, could not again reply;
Or fearing else some messenger, that might her mind
     discover,
Herself hath taught her love himself to write unto her
     lover.

160 All this I speak in print, for in print I found it. Why muse you, sir? 'Tis dinner-time.

VALENTINE I have dined.

SPEED Ay, but hearken, sir: though the chameleon Love can feed on the air, I am one that am nourished by my victuals, and would fain have meat. O, be not like your mistress; be moved, be moved.   *Exeunt*

Enter Proteus and Julia   II.2

PROTEUS

Have patience, gentle Julia.

JULIA

I must, where is no remedy.

PROTEUS

When possibly I can, I will return.

JULIA

If you turn not, you will return the sooner.
Keep this remembrance for thy Julia's sake.

She gives him a ring

PROTEUS

Why, then, we'll make exchange; here, take you this.

He gives her a ring

JULIA

And seal the bargain with a holy kiss.

PROTEUS

Here is my hand for my true constancy;
And when that hour o'erslips me in the day
Wherein I sigh not, Julia, for thy sake,   10
The next ensuing hour some foul mischance
Torment me for my love's forgetfulness!
My father stays my coming. Answer not.
The tide is now – nay, not thy tide of tears;
That tide will stay me longer than I should.
Julia, farewell. (*Exit Julia*) What, gone without a word?
Ay, so true love should do; it cannot speak,
For truth hath better deeds than words to grace it.

Enter Panthino

PANTHINO

Sir Proteus, you are stayed for.

PROTEUS   Go; I come.

(*Aside*) Alas, this parting strikes poor lovers dumb.   20

Exeunt

II.3   *Enter Launce with his dog, Crab*

LAUNCE Nay, 'twill be this hour ere I have done weeping; all the kind of the Launces have this very fault. I have received my proportion, like the prodigious son, and am going with Sir Proteus to the Imperial's court. I think Crab my dog be the sourest-natured dog that lives. My mother weeping, my father wailing, my sister crying, our maid howling, our cat wringing her hands, and all our house in a great perplexity; yet did not this cruel-hearted cur shed one tear. He is a stone, a very pebble-stone, and has no more pity in him than a dog. A Jew would have wept to have seen our parting. Why, my grandam, having no eyes, look you, wept herself blind at my parting. Nay, I'll show you the manner of it. This shoe is my father. No, this left shoe is my father. No, no, this left shoe is my mother. Nay, that cannot be so neither. Yes, it is so, it is so; it hath the worser sole. This shoe with the hole in it is my mother, and this my father. A vengeance on't, there 'tis. Now, sir, this staff is my sister; for, look you, she is as white as a lily, and as small as a wand. This hat is Nan our maid. I am the dog. No, the dog is himself, and I am the dog. O, the dog is me, and I am myself. Ay, so, so. Now come I to my father: 'Father, your blessing.' Now should not the shoe speak a word for weeping. Now should I kiss my father; well, he weeps on. Now come I to my mother. O, that she could speak now like an old woman! Well, I kiss her. Why, there 'tis; here's my mother's breath up and down. Now come I to my sister. Mark the moan she makes. Now the dog all this while sheds not a tear, nor speaks a word; but see how I lay the dust with my tears.

Enter Panthino

PANTHINO Launce, away, away! Aboard! Thy master is shipped, and thou art to post after with oars. What's the

matter? Why weepest thou, man? Away, ass, you'll lose
the tide, if you tarry any longer.

LAUNCE It is no matter if the tied were lost, for it is the
unkindest tied that ever any man tied.

PANTHINO What's the unkindest tide?

LAUNCE Why, he that's tied here, Crab, my dog.

PANTHINO Tut, man, I mean thou'lt lose the flood; and,
in losing the flood, lose thy voyage; and, in losing thy   40
voyage, lose thy master; and, in losing thy master, lose
thy service; and, in losing thy service – Why dost thou
stop my mouth?

LAUNCE For fear thou shouldst lose thy tongue.

PANTHINO Where should I lose my tongue?

LAUNCE In thy tale.

PANTHINO In my tail!

LAUNCE Lose the tide, and the voyage, and the master,
and the service, and the tied. Why, man, if the river
were dry, I am able to fill it with my tears. If the wind   50
were down, I could drive the boat with my sighs.

PANTHINO Come, come away, man. I was sent to call thee.

LAUNCE Sir, call me what thou darest.

PANTHINO Wilt thou go?

LAUNCE Well, I will go.   *Exeunt*

Enter Silvia, Thurio, Valentine, and Speed   II.4

SILVIA Servant!

VALENTINE Mistress?

SPEED (*to Valentine*) Master, Sir Thurio frowns on you.

VALENTINE (*to Speed*) Ay, boy; it's for love.

SPEED (*to Valentine*) Not of you.

VALENTINE (*to Speed*) Of my mistress, then.

SPEED (*to Valentine*) 'Twere good you knocked him.

                                                    Exit

SILVIA Servant, you are sad.

VALENTINE Indeed, madam, I seem so.

10 THURIO Seem you that you are not?

VALENTINE Haply I do.

THURIO So do counterfeits.

VALENTINE So do you.

THURIO What seem I that I am not?

VALENTINE Wise.

THURIO What instance of the contrary?

VALENTINE Your folly.

THURIO And how quote you my folly?

VALENTINE I quote it in your jerkin.

20 THURIO My jerkin is a doublet.

VALENTINE Well, then, I'll double your folly.

THURIO How?

SILVIA What, angry, Sir Thurio? Do you change colour?

VALENTINE Give him leave, madam; he is a kind of
    chameleon.

THURIO That hath more mind to feed on your blood than
    live in your air.

VALENTINE You have said, sir.

THURIO Ay, sir, and done too, for this time.

30 VALENTINE I know it well, sir; you always end ere you
    begin.

SILVIA A fine volley of words, gentlemen, and quickly
    shot off.

VALENTINE 'Tis indeed, madam. We thank the giver.

SILVIA Who is that, servant?

VALENTINE Yourself, sweet lady; for you gave the fire.
    Sir Thurio borrows his wit from your ladyship's looks,
    and spends what he borrows kindly in your company.

THURIO Sir, if you spend word for word with me, I shall
40   make your wit bankrupt.

VALENTINE I know it well, sir; you have an exchequer of

words, and, I think, no other treasure to give your fol-
lowers; for it appears by their bare liveries that they
live by your bare words.

Enter the Duke of Milan

SILVIA No more, gentlemen, no more! Here comes my
father.

DUKE

Now, daughter Silvia, you are hard beset.
Sir Valentine, your father is in good health.
What say you to a letter from your friends
Of much good news?

VALENTINE   My lord, I will be thankful   50
To any happy messenger from thence.

DUKE

Know ye Don Antonio, your countryman?

VALENTINE

Ay, my good lord, I know the gentleman
To be of worth, and worthy estimation,
And not without desert so well reputed.

DUKE

Hath he not a son?

VALENTINE

Ay, my good lord, a son that well deserves
The honour and regard of such a father.

DUKE

You know him well?

VALENTINE

I know him as myself; for from our infancy   60
We have conversed and spent our hours together;
And though myself have been an idle truant,
Omitting the sweet benefit of time
To clothe mine age with angel-like perfection,
Yet hath Sir Proteus – for that's his name –
Made use and fair advantage of his days:

His years but young, but his experience old;
His head unmellowed, but his judgement ripe;
And in a word, for far behind his worth
70 Comes all the praises that I now bestow,
He is complete in feature and in mind,
With all good grace to grace a gentleman.

DUKE
Beshrew me, sir, but if he make this good,
He is as worthy for an empress' love
As meet to be an emperor's counsellor.
Well, sir, this gentleman is come to me
With commendation from great potentates,
And here he means to spend his time awhile.
I think 'tis no unwelcome news to you.

VALENTINE
80 Should I have wished a thing, it had been he.

DUKE
Welcome him then according to his worth.
Silvia, I speak to you, and you, Sir Thurio;
For Valentine, I need not cite him to it.
I will send him hither to you presently.   *Exit*

VALENTINE
This is the gentleman I told your ladyship
Had come along with me but that his mistress
Did hold his eyes locked in her crystal looks.

SILVIA
Belike that now she hath enfranchised them
Upon some other pawn for fealty.

VALENTINE
90 Nay, sure, I think she holds them prisoners still.

SILVIA
Nay, then, he should be blind; and, being blind,
How could he see his way to seek out you?

VALENTINE
  Why, lady, Love hath twenty pair of eyes.

THURIO
  They say that Love hath not an eye at all.

VALENTINE
  To see such lovers, Thurio, as yourself;
  Upon a homely object Love can wink.
      Enter Proteus

SILVIA
  Have done, have done; here comes the gentleman.

VALENTINE
  Welcome, dear Proteus! Mistress, I beseech you
  Confirm his welcome with some special favour.

SILVIA
  His worth is warrant for his welcome hither,   100
  If this be he you oft have wished to hear from.

VALENTINE
  Mistress, it is. Sweet lady, entertain him
  To be my fellow-servant to your ladyship.

SILVIA
  Too low a mistress for so high a servant.

PROTEUS
  Not so, sweet lady; but too mean a servant
  To have a look of such a worthy mistress.

VALENTINE
  Leave off discourse of disability;
  Sweet lady, entertain him for your servant.

PROTEUS
  My duty will I boast of, nothing else.

SILVIA
  And duty never yet did want his meed.   110
  Servant, you are welcome to a worthless mistress.

PROTEUS
  I'll die on him that says so but yourself.

SILVIA

That you are welcome?

PROTEUS   That you are worthless.

Enter a Servant

SERVANT

Madam, my lord your father would speak with you.

SILVIA

I wait upon his pleasure. (*Exit Servant*) Come, Sir
    Thurio,
Go with me. Once more, new servant, welcome.
I'll leave you to confer of home affairs;
When you have done, we look to hear from you.

PROTEUS

We'll both attend upon your ladyship.

                              Exeunt Silvia and Thurio

VALENTINE

120   Now, tell me, how do all from whence you came?

PROTEUS

Your friends are well, and have them much com-
    mended.

VALENTINE

And how do yours?

PROTEUS   I left them all in health.

VALENTINE

How does your lady, and how thrives your love?

PROTEUS

My tales of love were wont to weary you;
I know you joy not in a love-discourse.

VALENTINE

Ay, Proteus, but that life is altered now;
I have done penance for contemning Love,
Whose high imperious thoughts have punished me
With bitter fasts, with penitential groans,

With nightly tears, and daily heart-sore sighs;   130
For, in revenge of my contempt of love,
Love hath chased sleep from my enthrallèd eyes,
And made them watchers of mine own heart's sorrow.
O gentle Proteus, Love's a mighty lord,
And hath so humbled me as I confess
There is no woe to his correction,
Nor to his service no such joy on earth.
Now no discourse, except it be of love;
Now can I break my fast, dine, sup, and sleep.
Upon the very naked name of love.   140

PROTEUS
Enough; I read your fortune in your eye.
Was this the idol that you worship so?

VALENTINE
Even she; and is she not a heavenly saint?

PROTEUS
No; but she is an earthly paragon.

VALENTINE
Call her divine.

PROTEUS   I will not flatter her.

VALENTINE
O, flatter me; for love delights in praises.

PROTEUS
When I was sick, you gave me bitter pills,
And I must minister the like to you.

VALENTINE
Then speak the truth by her; if not divine,
Yet let her be a principality,   150
Sovereign to all the creatures on the earth.

PROTEUS
Except my mistress.

VALENTINE   Sweet, except not any,

Except thou wilt except against my love.

PROTEUS

Have I not reason to prefer mine own?

VALENTINE

And I will help thee to prefer her too:
She shall be dignified with this high honour –
To bear my lady's train, lest the base earth
Should from her vesture chance to steal a kiss,
And, of so great a favour growing proud,
Disdain to root the summer-swelling flower
And make rough winter everlastingly.

PROTEUS

Why, Valentine, what braggardism is this?

VALENTINE

Pardon me, Proteus, all I can is nothing
To her, whose worth makes other worthies nothing;
She is alone.

PROTEUS   Then let her alone.

VALENTINE

Not for the world! Why, man, she is mine own;
And I as rich in having such a jewel
As twenty seas, if all their sand were pearl,
The water nectar, and the rocks pure gold.
Forgive me, that I do not dream on thee,
Because thou seest me dote upon my love.
My foolish rival, that her father likes
Only for his possessions are so huge,
Is gone with her along; and I must after,
For love, thou knowest, is full of jealousy.

PROTEUS

But she loves you?

VALENTINE

Ay, and we are betrothed; nay more, our marriage-
hour,

With all the cunning manner of our flight,
Determined of; how I must climb her window,
The ladder made of cords, and all the means   180
Plotted and 'greed on for my happiness.
Good Proteus, go with me to my chamber,
In these affairs to aid me with thy counsel.

PROTEUS

Go on before; I shall inquire you forth.
I must unto the road to disembark
Some necessaries that I needs must use;
And then I'll presently attend you.

VALENTINE

Will you make haste?

PROTEUS

I will.   *Exit Valentine*
Even as one heat another heat expels,   190
Or as one nail by strength drives out another,
So the remembrance of my former love
Is by a newer object quite forgotten.
Is it mine eye, or Valentine's praise,
Her true perfection, or my false transgression,
That makes me reasonless to reason thus?
She is fair; and so is Julia that I love –
That I did love, for now my love is thawed;
Which, like a waxen image 'gainst a fire,
Bears no impression of the thing it was.   200
Methinks my zeal to Valentine is cold,
And that I love him not as I was wont.
O, but I love his lady too too much!
And that's the reason I love him so little.
How shall I dote on her with more advice,
That thus without advice begin to love her!
'Tis but her picture I have yet beheld,
And that hath dazzlèd my reason's light;

But when I look on her perfections,
210   There is no reason but I shall be blind.
If I can check my erring love, I will;
If not, to compass her I'll use my skill.   *Exit*

II.5   *Enter Speed and Launce, meeting*

SPEED Launce! By mine honesty, welcome to Milan.

LAUNCE Forswear not thyself, sweet youth, for I am not
welcome. I reckon this always, that a man is never undone till he be hanged, nor never welcome to a place till
some certain shot be paid, and the hostess say, 'Welcome.'

SPEED Come on, you madcap; I'll to the alehouse with
you presently; where, for one shot of five pence, thou
shalt have five thousand welcomes. But, sirrah, how did
10   thy master part with Madam Julia?

LAUNCE Marry, after they closed in earnest, they parted
very fairly in jest.

SPEED But shall she marry him?

LAUNCE No.

SPEED How then? Shall he marry her?

LAUNCE No, neither.

SPEED What, are they broken?

LAUNCE No, they are both as whole as a fish.

SPEED Why then, how stands the matter with them?

20   LAUNCE Marry, thus: when it stands well with him, it
stands well with her.

SPEED What an ass art thou! I understand thee not.

LAUNCE What a block art thou, that thou canst not! My
staff understands me.

SPEED What thou sayest?

LAUNCE Ay, and what I do too; look there, I'll but lean,
and my staff understands me.

SPEED It stands under thee, indeed.

LAUNCE Why, stand-under and under-stand is all one.

SPEED But tell me true, will't be a match?   30

LAUNCE Ask my dog. If he say ay, it will; if he say no, it
will; if he shake his tail and say nothing, it will.

SPEED The conclusion is, then, that it will.

LAUNCE Thou shalt never get such a secret from me but
by a parable.

SPEED 'Tis well that I get it so. But, Launce, how sayest
thou that my master is become a notable lover?

LAUNCE I never knew him otherwise.

SPEED Than how?

LAUNCE A notable lubber, as thou reportest him to be.   40

SPEED Why, thou whoreson ass, thou mistakest me.

LAUNCE Why, fool, I meant not thee, I meant thy
master.

SPEED I tell thee my master is become a hot lover.

LAUNCE Why, I tell thee, I care not though he burn himself in love. If thou wilt, go with me to the alehouse; if
not, thou art an Hebrew, a Jew, and not worth the name
of a Christian.

SPEED Why?

LAUNCE Because thou hast not so much charity in thee as   50
to go to the ale with a Christian. Wilt thou go?

SPEED At thy service.   *Exeunt*

Enter Proteus   II.6

PROTEUS

To leave my Julia, shall I be forsworn;
To love fair Silvia, shall I be forsworn;
To wrong my friend, I shall be much forsworn.
And e'en that power which gave me first my oath
Provokes me to this threefold perjury:

Love bade me swear, and Love bids me forswear.
O sweet-suggesting Love, if thou hast sinned,
Teach me, thy tempted subject, to excuse it!
At first I did adore a twinkling star,
But now I worship a celestial sun.
Unheedful vows may heedfully be broken;
And he wants wit that wants resolvèd will
To learn his wit t'exchange the bad for better.
Fie, fie, unreverend tongue, to call her bad
Whose sovereignty so oft thou hast preferred
With twenty thousand soul-confirming oaths!
I cannot leave to love, and yet I do;
But there I leave to love where I should love.
Julia I lose, and Valentine I lose;
If I keep them, I needs must lose myself;
If I lose them, thus find I by their loss:
For Valentine, myself; for Julia, Silvia.
I to myself am dearer than a friend,
For love is still most precious in itself;
And Silvia – witness heaven, that made her fair! –
Shows Julia but a swarthy Ethiope.
I will forget that Julia is alive,
Remembering that my love to her is dead;
And Valentine I'll hold an enemy,
Aiming at Silvia as a sweeter friend.
I cannot now prove constant to myself
Without some treachery used to Valentine.
This night he meaneth with a corded ladder
To climb celestial Silvia's chamber-window,
Myself in counsel, his competitor.
Now presently I'll give her father notice
Of their disguising and pretended flight,
Who, all enraged, will banish Valentine,
For Thurio he intends shall wed his daughter;

But Valentine being gone, I'll quickly cross   40
By some sly trick blunt Thurio's dull proceeding.
Love, lend me wings to make my purpose swift,
As thou hast lent me wit to plot this drift!   *Exit*

Enter Julia and Lucetta   **II.7**

JULIA

Counsel, Lucetta; gentle girl, assist me;
And, e'en in kind love, I do conjure thee,
Who art the table wherein all my thoughts
Are visibly charactered and engraved,
To lesson me and tell me some good mean
How, with my honour, I may undertake
A journey to my loving Proteus.

LUCETTA

Alas, the way is wearisome and long!

JULIA

A true-devoted pilgrim is not weary
To measure kingdoms with his feeble steps;   10
Much less shall she that hath Love's wings to fly,
And when the flight is made to one so dear,
Of such divine perfection as Sir Proteus.

LUCETTA

Better forbear till Proteus make return.

JULIA

O, knowest thou not his looks are my soul's food?
Pity the dearth that I have pinèd in
By longing for that food so long a time.
Didst thou but know the inly touch of love,
Thou wouldst as soon go kindle fire with snow
As seek to quench the fire of love with words.   20

LUCETTA

I do not seek to quench your love's hot fire,

But qualify the fire's extreme rage,
Lest it should burn above the bounds of reason.

JULIA

The more thou dammest it up, the more it burns.
The current that with gentle murmur glides,
Thou knowest, being stopped, impatiently doth rage;
But when his fair course is not hinderèd,
He makes sweet music with th'enamelled stones,
Giving a gentle kiss to every sedge
30 He overtaketh in his pilgrimage;
And so by many winding nooks he strays,
With willing sport, to the wild ocean.
Then let me go, and hinder not my course.
I'll be as patient as a gentle stream,
And make a pastime of each weary step,
Till the last step have brought me to my love;
And there I'll rest as, after much turmoil,
A blessèd soul doth in Elysium.

LUCETTA

But in what habit will you go along?

JULIA

40 Not like a woman, for I would prevent
The loose encounters of lascivious men.
Gentle Lucetta, fit me with such weeds
As may beseem some well-reputed page.

LUCETTA

Why then, your ladyship must cut your hair.

JULIA

No, girl, I'll knit it up in silken strings
With twenty odd-conceited true-love knots –
To be fantastic may become a youth
Of greater time than I shall show to be.

LUCETTA

What fashion, madam, shall I make your breeches?

JULIA

That fits as well as, 'Tell me, good my lord,   50
What compass will you wear your farthingale?'
Why e'en what fashion thou best likes, Lucetta.

LUCETTA

You must needs have them with a codpiece, madam.

JULIA

Out, out, Lucetta, that will be ill-favoured.

LUCETTA

A round hose, madam, now's not worth a pin,
Unless you have a codpiece to stick pins on.

JULIA

Lucetta, as thou lovest me, let me have
What thou thinkest meet, and is most mannerly.
But tell me, wench, how will the world repute me
For undertaking so unstaid a journey?   60
I fear me it will make me scandalized.

LUCETTA

If you think so, then stay at home and go not.

JULIA

Nay, that I will not.

LUCETTA

Then never dream on infamy, but go.
If Proteus like your journey when you come,
No matter who's displeased when you are gone.
I fear me he will scarce be pleased withal.

JULIA

That is the least, Lucetta, of my fear:
A thousand oaths, an ocean of his tears,
And instances of infinite of love,   70
Warrant me welcome to my Proteus.

LUCETTA

All these are servants to deceitful men.

JULIA

    Base men, that use them to so base effect!
    But truer stars did govern Proteus' birth;
    His words are bonds, his oaths are oracles,
    His love sincere, his thoughts immaculate,
    His tears pure messengers sent from his heart,
    His heart as far from fraud as heaven from earth.

LUCETTA

    Pray heaven he prove so when you come to him!

JULIA

80   Now, as thou lovest me, do him not that wrong
    To bear a hard opinion of his truth;
    Only deserve my love by loving him;
    And presently go with me to my chamber,
    To take a note of what I stand in need of
    To furnish me upon my longing journey.
    All that is mine I leave at thy dispose,
    My goods, my land, my reputation;
    Only, in lieu thereof, dispatch me hence.
    Come, answer not, but to it presently;
90   I am impatient of my tarriance.   *Exeunt*

*

III.1   *Enter the Duke of Milan, Thurio, and Proteus*

DUKE

    Sir Thurio, give us leave, I pray, awhile;
    We have some secrets to confer about.   *Exit Thurio*
    Now, tell me, Proteus, what's your will with me?

PROTEUS

    My gracious lord, that which I would discover
    The law of friendship bids me to conceal,
    But when I call to mind your gracious favours

Done to me, undeserving as I am,
My duty pricks me on to utter that
Which else no worldly good should draw from me.
Know, worthy prince, Sir Valentine, my friend,   10
This night intends to steal away your daughter;
Myself am one made privy to the plot.
I know you have determined to bestow her
On Thurio, whom your gentle daughter hates;
And should she thus be stolen away from you,
It would be much vexation to your age.
Thus, for my duty's sake, I rather chose
To cross my friend in his intended drift
Than, by concealing it, heap on your head
A pack of sorrows which would press you down,   20
Being unprevented, to your timeless grave.

DUKE

Proteus, I thank thee for thine honest care,
Which to requite, command me while I live.
This love of theirs myself have often seen,
Haply when they have judged me fast asleep,
And oftentimes have purposed to forbid
Sir Valentine her company and my court;
But, fearing lest my jealous aim might err,
And so, unworthily, disgrace the man –
A rashness that I ever yet have shunned –   30
I gave him gentle looks, thereby to find
That which thyself hast now disclosed to me.
And, that thou mayst perceive my fear of this,
Knowing that tender youth is soon suggested,
I nightly lodge her in an upper tower,
The key whereof myself have ever kept;
And thence she cannot be conveyed away.

PROTEUS

Know, noble lord, they have devised a mean

How he her chamber-window will ascend
40 And with a corded ladder fetch her down;
For which the youthful lover now is gone,
And this way comes he with it presently;
Where, if it please you, you may intercept him.
But, good my lord, do it so cunningly
That my discovery be not aimèd at;
For, love of you, not hate unto my friend,
Hath made me publisher of this pretence.

DUKE

Upon mine honour, he shall never know
That I had any light from thee of this.

PROTEUS

50 Adieu, my lord, Sir Valentine is coming.   *Exit*
    Enter Valentine

DUKE

Sir Valentine, whither away so fast?

VALENTINE

Please it your grace, there is a messenger
That stays to bear my letters to my friends,
And I am going to deliver them.

DUKE

Be they of much import?

VALENTINE

The tenor of them doth but signify
My health and happy being at your court.

DUKE

Nay then, no matter; stay with me awhile;
I am to break with thee of some affairs
60 That touch me near, wherein thou must be secret.
'Tis not unknown to thee that I have sought
To match my friend Sir Thurio to my daughter.

VALENTINE

I know it well, my lord; and, sure, the match

Were rich and honourable; besides, the gentleman
Is full of virtue, bounty, worth, and qualities
Beseeming such a wife as your fair daughter.
Cannot your grace win her to fancy him?

DUKE

No, trust me; she is peevish, sullen, froward,
Proud, disobedient, stubborn, lacking duty;
Neither regarding that she is my child,   70
Nor fearing me as if I were her father;
And, may I say to thee, this pride of hers,
Upon advice, hath drawn my love from her;
And where I thought the remnant of mine age
Should have been cherished by her child-like duty,
I now am full resolved to take a wife
And turn her out to who will take her in.
Then let her beauty be her wedding-dower;
For me and my possessions she esteems not.

VALENTINE

What would your grace have me to do in this?   80

DUKE

There is a lady of Verona here
Whom I affect; but she is nice, and coy,
And naught esteems my agèd eloquence.
Now, therefore, would I have thee to my tutor –
For long agone I have forgot to court;
Besides, the fashion of the time is changed –
How and which way I may bestow myself
To be regarded in her sun-bright eye.

VALENTINE

Win her with gifts, if she respect not words;
Dumb jewels often in their silent kind   90
More than quick words do move a woman's mind.

DUKE

But she did scorn a present that I sent her.

VALENTINE

A woman sometime scorns what best contents her.
Send her another; never give her o'er;
For scorn at first makes after-love the more.
If she do frown, 'tis not in hate of you,
But rather to beget more love in you;
If she do chide, 'tis not to have you gone,
For why, the fools are mad if left alone.
Take no repulse, whatever she doth say;
For 'Get you gone', she doth not mean 'Away!'
Flatter and praise, commend, extol their graces;
Though ne'er so black, say they have angels' faces.
That man that hath a tongue, I say, is no man,
If with his tongue he cannot win a woman.

DUKE

But she I mean is promised by her friends
Unto a youthful gentleman of worth;
And kept severely from resort of men,
That no man hath access by day to her.

VALENTINE

Why then, I would resort to her by night.

DUKE

Ay, but the doors be locked, and keys kept safe,
That no man hath recourse to her by night.

VALENTINE

What lets but one may enter at her window?

DUKE

Her chamber is aloft, far from the ground,
And built so shelving that one cannot climb it
Without apparent hazard of his life.

VALENTINE

Why then, a ladder, quaintly made of cords,
To cast up with a pair of anchoring hooks,
Would serve to scale another Hero's tower,

So bold Leander would adventure it.   120

DUKE

Now, as thou art a gentleman of blood,
Advise me where I may have such a ladder.

VALENTINE

When would you use it? Pray, sir, tell me that.

DUKE

This very night; for Love is like a child,
That longs for every thing that he can come by.

VALENTINE

By seven o'clock I'll get you such a ladder.

DUKE

But, hark thee; I will go to her alone;
How shall I best convey the ladder thither?

VALENTINE

It will be light, my lord, that you may bear it
Under a cloak that is of any length.   130

DUKE

A cloak as long as thine will serve the turn?

VALENTINE

Ay, my good lord.

DUKE   Then let me see thy cloak;
I'll get me one of such another length.

VALENTINE

Why, any cloak will serve the turn, my lord.

DUKE

How shall I fashion me to wear a cloak?
I pray thee, let me feel thy cloak upon me.

  *He lifts Valentine's cloak and finds a letter and a
  rope-ladder*

What letter is this same? What's here? *To Silvia*!
And here an engine fit for my proceeding.
I'll be so bold to break the seal for once.

  (*He opens the letter and reads*)

140 *My thoughts do harbour with my Silvia nightly,*
  And slaves they are to me, that send them flying.
O, could their master come and go as lightly,
  Himself would lodge where, senseless, they are lying!
My herald thoughts in thy pure bosom rest them,
  While I, their king, that thither them importune,
Do curse the grace that with such grace hath blessed them,
  Because myself do want my servants' fortune.
I curse myself, for they are sent by me,
That they should harbour where their lord should be.
150 What's here?
Silvia, this night I will enfranchise thee.
'Tis so; and here's the ladder for the purpose.
Why, Phaethon – for thou art Merops' son –
Wilt thou aspire to guide the heavenly car,
And with thy daring folly burn the world?
Wilt thou reach stars, because they shine on thee?
Go, base intruder, overweening slave,
Bestow thy fawning smiles on equal mates;
And think my patience, more than thy desert,
160 Is privilege for thy departure hence.
Thank me for this more than for all the favours
Which, all too much, I have bestowed on thee.
But if thou linger in my territories
Longer than swiftest expedition
Will give thee time to leave our royal court,
By heaven, my wrath shall far exceed the love
I ever bore my daughter or thyself.
Be gone; I will not hear thy vain excuse,
But, as thou lovest thy life, make speed from hence.
                                                        Exit

VALENTINE
170 And why not death, rather than living torment?

To die is to be banished from myself,
And Silvia is myself; banished from her
Is self from self – a deadly banishment.
What light is light, if Silvia be not seen?
What joy is joy, if Silvia be not by?
Unless it be to think that she is by,
And feed upon the shadow of perfection.
Except I be by Silvia in the night,
There is no music in the nightingale;
Unless I look on Silvia in the day,   180
There is no day for me to look upon.
She is my essence, and I leave to be,
If I be not by her fair influence
Fostered, illumined, cherished, kept alive.
I fly not death, to fly his deadly doom:
Tarry I here, I but attend on death;
But fly I hence, I fly away from life.

    Enter Proteus and Launce

PROTEUS Run, boy, run, run, and seek him out.
LAUNCE So-ho, so-ho!
PROTEUS What seest thou?   190
LAUNCE Him we go to find: there's not a hair on's head
    but 'tis a Valentine.
PROTEUS Valentine?
VALENTINE No.
PROTEUS Who then? His spirit?
VALENTINE Neither.
PROTEUS What then?
VALENTINE Nothing.
LAUNCE Can nothing speak? Master, shall I strike?
PROTEUS Who wouldst thou strike?   200
LAUNCE Nothing.
PROTEUS Villain, forbear.

LAUNCE Why, sir, I'll strike nothing. I pray you —

PROTEUS

Sirrah, I say forbear. Friend Valentine, a word.

VALENTINE

My ears are stopped and cannot hear good news,
So much of bad already hath possessed them.

PROTEUS

Then in dumb silence will I bury mine,
For they are harsh, untuneable, and bad.

VALENTINE

Is Silvia dead?

PROTEUS

210   No, Valentine.

VALENTINE

No Valentine, indeed, for sacred Silvia.
Hath she forsworn me?

PROTEUS

No, Valentine.

VALENTINE

No Valentine, if Silvia have forsworn me.
What is your news?

LAUNCE Sir, there is a proclamation that you are vanished.

PROTEUS

That thou art banishèd — O, that's the news! —
From hence, from Silvia, and from me thy friend.

VALENTINE

O, I have fed upon this woe already,
220   And now excess of it will make me surfeit.
Doth Silvia know that I am banishèd?

PROTEUS

Ay, ay; and she hath offered to the doom —
Which, unreversed, stands in effectual force —
A sea of melting pearl, which some call tears;
Those at her father's churlish feet she tendered;

With them, upon her knees, her humble self,
Wringing her hands, whose whiteness so became them
As if but now they waxèd pale for woe.
But neither bended knees, pure hands held up,
Sad sighs, deep groans, nor silver-shedding tears,   230
Could penetrate her uncompassionate sire –
But Valentine, if he be ta'en, must die.
Besides, her intercession chafed him so,
When she for thy repeal was suppliant,
That to close prison he commanded her,
With many bitter threats of biding there.

VALENTINE

No more; unless the next word that thou speakest
Have some malignant power upon my life;
If so, I pray thee breathe it in mine ear,
As ending anthem of my endless dolour.   230

PROTEUS

Cease to lament for that thou canst not help,
And study help for that which thou lamentest.
Time is the nurse and breeder of all good;
Here, if thou stay, thou canst not see thy love;
Besides, thy staying will abridge thy life.
Hope is a lover's staff; walk hence with that,
And manage it against despairing thoughts.
Thy letters may be here, though thou art hence,
Which, being writ to me, shall be delivered
Even in the milk-white bosom of thy love.   250
The time now serves not to expostulate.
Come I'll convey thee through the city gate;
And, ere I part with thee, confer at large
Of all that may concern thy love affairs.
As thou lovest Silvia, though not for thyself,
Regard thy danger, and along with me.

VALENTINE

I pray thee, Launce, an if thou seest my boy,
Bid him make haste and meet me at the Northgate.

PROTEUS

Go, sirrah, find him out. Come, Valentine.

VALENTINE

260   O my dear Silvia! Hapless Valentine!

Exeunt Valentine and Proteus

LAUNCE I am but a fool, look you, and yet I have the wit to
think my master is a kind of a knave; but that's all one
if he be but one knave. He lives not now that knows me
to be in love; yet I am in love; but a team of horse shall
not pluck that from me; nor who 'tis I love; and yet 'tis
a woman; but what woman I will not tell myself; and
yet 'tis a milkmaid; yet 'tis not a maid, for she hath had
gossips; yet 'tis a maid, for she is her master's maid and
serves for wages. She hath more qualities than a water-
270   spaniel – which is much in a bare Christian.

He produces a paper

Here is the cate-log of her condition. *Imprimis: She can
fetch and carry.* Why, a horse can do no more; nay, a
horse cannot fetch, but only carry; therefore is she better
than a jade. *Item: She can milk.* Look you, a sweet
virtue in a maid with clean hands.

Enter Speed

SPEED How now, Signior Launce? What news with your
mastership?

LAUNCE With my master's ship? Why, it is at sea.

SPEED Well, your old vice still: mistake the word. What
280   news, then, in your paper?

LAUNCE The blackest news that ever thou heardest.

SPEED Why, man? How black?

LAUNCE Why, as black as ink.

SPEED Let me read them.

LAUNCE Fie on thee, jolt-head; thou canst not read.

SPEED Thou liest; I can.

LAUNCE I will try thee. Tell me this: who begot thee?

SPEED Marry, the son of my grandfather.

LAUNCE O illiterate loiterer! It was the son of thy grandmother. This proves that thou canst not read.   290

SPEED Come, fool, come; try me in thy paper.

LAUNCE There; and Saint Nicholas be thy speed!

He hands over the paper from which Speed reads

SPEED *Imprimis: She can milk.*

LAUNCE Ay, that she can.

SPEED *Item: She brews good ale.*

LAUNCE And thereof comes the proverb: 'Blessing of your
heart, you brew good ale.'

SPEED *Item: She can sew.*

LAUNCE That's as much as to say, 'Can she so?'

SPEED *Item: She can knit.*   300

LAUNCE What need a man care for a stock with a wench,
when she can knit him a stock?

SPEED *Item: She can wash and scour.*

LAUNCE A special virtue; for then she need not be
washed and scoured.

SPEED *Item: She can spin.*

LAUNCE Then may I set the world on wheels, when she
can spin for her living.

SPEED *Item: She hath many nameless virtues.*

LAUNCE That's as much as to say, bastard virtues; that   310
indeed know not their fathers, and therefore have no
names.

SPEED Here follow her vices.

LAUNCE Close at the heels of her virtues.

SPEED *Item: She is not to be kissed fasting, in respect of her
breath.*

LAUNCE Well, that fault may be mended with a breakfast. Read on.

SPEED *Item: She hath a sweet mouth.*

320 LAUNCE That makes amends for her sour breath.

SPEED *Item: She doth talk in her sleep.*

LAUNCE It's no matter for that; so she sleep not in her talk.

SPEED *Item: She is slow in words.*

LAUNCE O villain, that set this down among her vices! To be slow in words is a woman's only virtue. I pray thee, out with't, and place it for her chief virtue.

SPEED *Item: She is proud.*

LAUNCE Out with that too; it was Eve's legacy, and can-
330 not be ta'en from her.

SPEED *Item: She hath no teeth.*

LAUNCE I care not for that neither, because I love crusts.

SPEED *Item: She is curst.*

LAUNCE Well, the best is, she hath no teeth to bite.

SPEED *Item: She will often praise her liquor.*

LAUNCE If her liquor be good, she shall; if she will not, I will; for good things should be praised.

SPEED *Item: She is too liberal.*

LAUNCE Of her tongue she cannot, for that's writ down
340 she is slow of; of her purse, she shall not, for that I'll keep shut. Now, of another thing she may, and that cannot I help. Well, proceed.

SPEED *Item: She hath more hair than wit, and more faults than hairs, and more wealth than faults.*

LAUNCE Stop there; I'll have her; she was mine and not mine twice or thrice in that last article. Rehearse that once more.

SPEED *Item: She hath more hair than wit —*

LAUNCE More hair than wit? It may be I'll prove it: the
350 cover of the salt hides the salt, and therefore it is more

than the salt; the hair that covers the wit is more than
the wit, for the greater hides the less. What's next?

SPEED *And more faults than hairs –*

LAUNCE That's monstrous. O, that that were out!

SPEED *And more wealth than faults.*

LAUNCE Why, that word makes the faults gracious. Well,
I'll have her; an if it be a match, as nothing is impossible –

SPEED What then?

LAUNCE Why, then will I tell thee – that thy master stays   360
for thee at the Northgate.

SPEED For me?

LAUNCE For thee! Ay, who art thou? He hath stayed for
a better man than thee.

SPEED And must I go to him?

LAUNCE Thou must run to him, for thou hast stayed so
long that going will scarce serve the turn.

SPEED Why didst not tell me sooner? Pox of your love
letters!   *He returns the paper to Launce. Exit*

LAUNCE Now will he be swinged for reading my letter.   370
An unmannerly slave, that will thrust himself into
secrets! I'll after, to rejoice in the boy's correction.

Exit

Enter the Duke of Milan and Thurio   III.2

DUKE
Sir Thurio, fear not but that she will love you
Now Valentine is banished from her sight.

THURIO
Since his exile she hath despised me most,
Forsworn my company, and railed at me,
That I am desperate of obtaining her.

DUKE

This weak impress of love is as a figure
Trenchèd in ice, which with an hour's heat
Dissolves to water, and doth lose his form.
A little time will melt her frozen thoughts,
And worthless Valentine shall be forgot.

10

Enter Proteus

How now, Sir Proteus? Is your countryman,
According to our proclamation, gone?

PROTEUS

Gone, my good lord.

DUKE

My daughter takes his going grievously.

PROTEUS

A little time, my lord, will kill that grief.

DUKE

So I believe; but Thurio thinks not so.
Proteus, the good conceit I hold of thee –
For thou hast shown some sign of good desert –
Makes me the better to confer with thee.

PROTEUS

20

Longer than I prove loyal to your grace
Let me not live to look upon your grace.

DUKE

Thou knowest how willingly I would effect
The match between Sir Thurio and my daughter?

PROTEUS

I do, my lord.

DUKE

And also, I think, thou art not ignorant
How she opposes her against my will?

PROTEUS

She did, my lord, when Valentine was here.

DUKE

Ay, and perversely she persevers so.
What might we do to make the girl forget
The love of Valentine, and love Sir Thurio?   30

PROTEUS

The best way is to slander Valentine,
With falsehood, cowardice, and poor descent –
Three things that women highly hold in hate.

DUKE

Ay, but she'll think that it is spoke in hate.

PROTEUS

Ay, if his enemy deliver it;
Therefore it must with circumstance be spoken
By one whom she esteemeth as his friend.

DUKE

Then you must undertake to slander him.

PROTEUS

And that, my lord, I shall be loath to do:
'Tis an ill office for a gentleman,   40
Especially against his very friend.

DUKE

Where your good word cannot advantage him,
Your slander never can endamage him;
Therefore the office is indifferent,
Being entreated to it by your friend.

PROTEUS

You have prevailed, my lord; if I can do it
By aught that I can speak in his dispraise,
She shall not long continue love to him.
But say this weed her love from Valentine,
It follows not that she will love Sir Thurio.   50

THURIO

Therefore, as you unwind her love from him,

Lest it should ravel, and be good to none,
You must provide to bottom it on me;
Which must be done by praising me as much
As you in worth dispraise Sir Valentine.

DUKE

And, Proteus, we dare trust you in this kind,
Because we know, on Valentine's report,
You are already Love's firm votary,
And cannot soon revolt and change your mind.
Upon this warrant shall you have access
Where you with Silvia may confer at large –
For she is lumpish, heavy, melancholy,
And, for your friend's sake, will be glad of you –
Where you may temper her, by your persuasion,
To hate young Valentine and love my friend.

PROTEUS

As much as I can do I will effect.
But you, Sir Thurio, are not sharp enough;
You must lay lime to tangle her desires
By wailful sonnets, whose composèd rhymes
Should be full-fraught with serviceable vows.

DUKE

Ay,
Much is the force of heaven-bred poesy.

PROTEUS

Say that upon the altar of her beauty
You sacrifice your tears, your sighs, your heart;
Write till your ink be dry, and with your tears
Moist it again, and frame some feeling line
That may discover such integrity;
For Orpheus' lute was strung with poets' sinews,
Whose golden touch could soften steel and stones,
Make tigers tame, and huge leviathans
Forsake unsounded deeps to dance on sands.

After your dire-lamenting elegies,
Visit by night your lady's chamber-window
With some sweet consort; to their instruments
Tune a deploring dump – the night's dead silence
Will well become such sweet complaining grievance.
This, or else nothing, will inherit her.

DUKE

This discipline shows thou hast been in love.

THURIO

And thy advice this night I'll put in practice;
Therefore, sweet Proteus, my direction-giver,   90
Let us into the city presently
To sort some gentlemen well skilled in music.
I have a sonnet that will serve the turn
To give the onset to thy good advice.

DUKE

About it, gentlemen!

PROTEUS

We'll wait upon your grace till after supper,
And afterward determine our proceedings.

DUKE

Even now about it! I will pardon you.   *Exeunt*

*

Enter certain Outlaws   IV.1

FIRST OUTLAW

Fellows, stand fast; I see a passenger.

SECOND OUTLAW

If there be ten, shrink not, but down with 'em.
   Enter Valentine and Speed

THIRD OUTLAW

Stand, sir, and throw us that you have about ye;

If not, we'll make you sit, and rifle you.

SPEED
Sir, we are undone; these are the villains
That all the travellers do fear so much.

VALENTINE
My friends —

FIRST OUTLAW
That's not so, sir; we are your enemies.

SECOND OUTLAW
Peace! We'll hear him.

THIRD OUTLAW
10   Ay, by my beard, will we; for he's a proper man.

VALENTINE
Then know that I have little wealth to lose;
A man I am crossed with adversity;
My riches are these poor habiliments,
Of which, if you should here disfurnish me,
You take the sum and substance that I have.

SECOND OUTLAW
Whither travel you?

VALENTINE
To Verona.

FIRST OUTLAW
Whence came you?

VALENTINE
From Milan.

THIRD OUTLAW Have you long sojourned there?

VALENTINE
20   Some sixteen months, and longer might have stayed,
If crooked fortune had not thwarted me.

FIRST OUTLAW
What, were you banished thence?

VALENTINE
I was.

SECOND OUTLAW
  For what offence?
VALENTINE
  For that which now torments me to rehearse:
  I killed a man, whose death I much repent;
  But yet I slew him manfully in fight,
  Without false vantage or base treachery.
FIRST OUTLAW
  Why, ne'er repent it, if it were done so.
  But were you banished for so small a fault?   30
VALENTINE
  I was, and held me glad of such a doom.
SECOND OUTLAW
  Have you the tongues?
VALENTINE
  My youthful travel therein made me happy,
  Or else I often had been miserable.
THIRD OUTLAW
  By the bare scalp of Robin Hood's fat friar,
  This fellow were a king for our wild faction!
FIRST OUTLAW
  We'll have him. Sirs, a word.
      The Outlaws draw aside to talk
SPEED Master, be one of them; it's an honourable kind of
  thievery.
VALENTINE
  Peace, villain!   40
SECOND OUTLAW Tell us this: have you anything to take
  to?
VALENTINE
  Nothing but my fortune.
THIRD OUTLAW
  Know then that some of us are gentlemen,
  Such as the fury of ungoverned youth

Thrust from the company of awful men;
Myself was from Verona banishèd
For practising to steal away a lady,
An heir, and near allied unto the Duke.

SECOND OUTLAW

50 And I from Mantua, for a gentleman
Who, in my mood, I stabbed unto the heart.

FIRST OUTLAW

And I for such like petty crimes as these.
But to the purpose – for we cite our faults
That they may hold excused our lawless lives;
And partly, seeing you are beautified
With goodly shape, and by your own report
A linguist, and a man of such perfection
As we do in our quality much want –

SECOND OUTLAW

Indeed, because you are a banished man,
60 Therefore, above the rest, we parley to you.
Are you content to be our general –
To make a virtue of necessity,
And live as we do in this wilderness?

THIRD OUTLAW

What sayst thou? Wilt thou be of our consort?
Say 'ay', and be the captain of us all.
We'll do thee homage, and be ruled by thee,
Love thee as our commander and our king.

FIRST OUTLAW

But if thou scorn our courtesy, thou diest.

SECOND OUTLAW

Thou shalt not live to brag what we have offered.

VALENTINE

70 I take your offer, and will live with you,
Provided that you do no outrages
On silly women or poor passengers.

THIRD OUTLAW

    No, we detest such vile base practices.
    Come, go with us; we'll bring thee to our crews,
    And show thee all the treasure we have got;
    Which, with ourselves, all rest at thy dispose. *Exeunt*

    Enter Proteus   IV.2

PROTEUS

    Already have I been false to Valentine,
    And now I must be as unjust to Thurio;
    Under the colour of commending him,
    I have access my own love to prefer;
    But Silvia is too fair, too true, too holy,
    To be corrupted with my worthless gifts.
    When I protest true loyalty to her,
    She twits me with my falsehood to my friend;
    When to her beauty I commend my vows,
    She bids me think how I have been forsworn   10
    In breaking faith with Julia, whom I loved;
    And notwithstanding all her sudden quips,
    The least whereof would quell a lover's hope,
    Yet, spaniel-like, the more she spurns my love
    The more it grows and fawneth on her still.
    Enter Thurio and Musicians
    But here comes Thurio. Now must we to her window,
    And give some evening music to her ear.

THURIO

    How now, Sir Proteus, are you crept before us?

PROTEUS

    Ay, gentle Thurio; for you know that love
    Will creep in service where it cannot go.   20

THURIO

    Ay, but I hope, sir, that you love not here.

PROTEUS

Sir, but I do; or else I would be hence.

THURIO

Who? Silvia?

PROTEUS   Ay, Silvia – for your sake.

THURIO

I thank you for your own. Now, gentlemen,
Let's tune, and to it lustily awhile.

*Enter, some way off, the Host of the Inn, and Julia in
a page's costume*

HOST Now, my young guest, methinks you're allycholly;
I pray you, why is it?

JULIA Marry, mine host, because I cannot be merry.

HOST Come, we'll have you merry; I'll bring you where
you shall hear music, and see the gentleman that you
asked for.

JULIA But shall I hear him speak?

HOST Ay, that you shall.

JULIA That will be music.

The Musicians play

HOST Hark, hark!

JULIA Is he among these?

HOST Ay; but, peace! Let's hear 'em.

Song

Who is Silvia? What is she,
    That all our swains commend her?
Holy, fair, and wise is she;
    The heaven such grace did lend her,
That she might admirèd be.

Is she kind as she is fair?
    For beauty lives with kindness.

Love doth to her eyes repair,
   To help him of his blindness;
And, being helped, inhabits there.

Then to Silvia let us sing
   That Silvia is excelling;
She excels each mortal thing   50
   Upon the dull earth dwelling.
To her let us garlands bring.

HOST How now? Are you sadder than you were before?
   How do you, man? The music likes you not.
JULIA You mistake; the musician likes me not.
HOST Why, my pretty youth?
JULIA He plays false, father.
HOST How? Out of tune on the strings?
JULIA Not so; but yet so false that he grieves my very
   heart-strings.   60
HOST You have a quick ear.
JULIA Ay, I would I were deaf; it makes me have a slow
   heart.
HOST I perceive you delight not in music.
JULIA Not a whit, when it jars so.
HOST Hark, what fine change is in the music!
JULIA Ay; that change is the spite.
HOST You would have them always play but one thing?
JULIA
   I would always have one play but one thing.
   But, host, doth this Sir Proteus, that we talk on,   70
   Often resort unto this gentlewoman?
HOST I tell you what Launce, his man, told me: he loved
   her out of all nick.
JULIA Where is Launce?

HOST Gone to seek his dog, which tomorrow, by his
    master's command, he must carry for a present to his
    lady.

JULIA
    Peace! Stand aside; the company parts.

PROTEUS
    Sir Thurio, fear not you; I will so plead
80 That you shall say my cunning drift excels.

THURIO
    Where meet we?

PROTEUS   At Saint Gregory's Well.

THURIO   Farewell.
                        Exeunt Thurio and Musicians
        Enter Silvia at an upstairs window

PROTEUS
    Madam, good even to your ladyship.

SILVIA
    I thank you for your music, gentlemen.
    Who is that that spake?

PROTEUS
    One, lady, if you knew his pure heart's truth,
    You would quickly learn to know him by his voice.

SILVIA
    Sir Proteus, as I take it.

PROTEUS
    Sir Proteus, gentle lady, and your servant.

SILVIA
    What's your will?

PROTEUS   That I may compass yours.

SILVIA
90 You have your wish; my will is even this,
    That presently you hie you home to bed.
    Thou subtle, perjured, false, disloyal man,
    Thinkest thou I am so shallow, so conceitless,

To be seducèd by thy flattery
That hast deceived so many with thy vows?
Return, return, and make thy love amends.
For me – by this pale queen of night I swear –
I am so far from granting thy request
That I despise thee for thy wrongful suit;
And by and by intend to chide myself   100
Even for this time I spend in talking to thee.

PROTEUS

I grant, sweet love, that I did love a lady,
But she is dead.

JULIA (*aside*)   'Twere false, if I should speak it;
For I am sure she is not burièd.

SILVIA

Say that she be; yet Valentine thy friend
Survives, to whom, thyself art witness,
I am betrothed; and art thou not ashamed
To wrong him with thy importunacy?

PROTEUS

I likewise hear that Valentine is dead.

SILVIA

And so suppose am I; for in his grave   110
Assure thyself my love is burièd.

PROTEUS

Sweet lady, let me rake it from the earth.

SILVIA

Go to thy lady's grave and call hers thence;
Or, at the least, in hers sepulchre thine.

JULIA (*aside*)

He heard not that.

PROTEUS

Madam, if your heart be so obdurate,
Vouchsafe me yet your picture for my love,
The picture that is hanging in your chamber;

To that I'll speak, to that I'll sigh and weep;
120   For since the substance of your perfect self
Is else devoted, I am but a shadow;
And to your shadow will I make true love.

JULIA (*aside*)
If 'twere a substance, you would sure deceive it
And make it but a shadow, as I am.

SILVIA
I am very loath to be your idol, sir;
But, since your falsehood shall become you well
To worship shadows and adore false shapes,
Send to me in the morning and I'll send it;
And so, good rest.

PROTEUS   As wretches have o'ernight
130   That wait for execution in the morn.

                              Exeunt Proteus and Silvia

JULIA Host, will you go?
HOST By my halidom, I was fast asleep.
JULIA Pray you, where lies Sir Proteus?
HOST Marry, at my house. Trust me, I think 'tis almost
    day.
JULIA
Not so; but it hath been the longest night
That e'er I watched, and the most heaviest.   *Exeunt*

IV.3

        Enter Eglamour
EGLAMOUR
This is the hour that Madam Silvia
Entreated me to call and know her mind;
There's some great matter she'd employ me in.
Madam, madam!
        Enter Silvia at an upstairs window

SILVIA   Who calls?
EGLAMOUR   Your servant and your friend;
  One that attends your ladyship's command.
SILVIA
  Sir Eglamour, a thousand times good morrow.
EGLAMOUR
  As many, worthy lady, to yourself!
  According to your ladyship's impose,
  I am thus early come, to know what service
  It is your pleasure to command me in.   10
SILVIA
  O Eglamour, thou art a gentleman —
  Think not I flatter, for I swear I do not —
  Valiant, wise, remorseful, well-accomplished.
  Thou art not ignorant what dear good will
  I bear unto the banished Valentine;
  Nor how my father would enforce me marry
  Vain Thurio, whom my very soul abhors.
  Thyself hast loved, and I have heard thee say
  No grief did ever come so near thy heart
  As when thy lady and thy true love died,   20
  Upon whose grave thou vowedst pure chastity.
  Sir Eglamour, I would to Valentine,
  To Mantua, where I hear he makes abode;
  And, for the ways are dangerous to pass,
  I do desire thy worthy company,
  Upon whose faith and honour I repose.
  Urge not my father's anger, Eglamour,
  But think upon my grief, a lady's grief,
  And on the justice of my flying hence,
  To keep me from a most unholy match,   30
  Which heaven and fortune still rewards with plagues.
  I do desire thee, even from a heart

As full of sorrows as the sea of sands,
To bear me company and go with me;
If not, to hide what I have said to thee,
That I may venture to depart alone.

EGLAMOUR
Madam, I pity much your grievances;
Which since I know they virtuously are placed,
I give consent to go along with you,
40   Recking as little what betideth me
As much I wish all good befortune you.
When will you go?

SILVIA   This evening coming.

EGLAMOUR
Where shall I meet you?

SILVIA   At Friar Patrick's cell,
Where I intend holy confession.

EGLAMOUR I will not fail your ladyship. Good morrow,
gentle lady.

SILVIA Good morrow, kind Sir Eglamour.   *Exeunt*

IV.4   *Enter Launce, with his dog*

LAUNCE When a man's servant shall play the cur with
him, look you, it goes hard – one that I brought up of a
puppy; one that I saved from drowning, when three or
four of his blind brothers and sisters went to it. I have
taught him, even as one would say precisely, 'Thus I
would teach a dog.' I was sent to deliver him as a present
to Mistress Silvia from my master; and I came no sooner
into the dining-chamber, but he steps me to her
trencher and steals her capon's leg. O, 'tis a foul thing
10   when a cur cannot keep himself in all companies! I
would have, as one should say, one that takes upon him
to be a dog indeed, to be, as it were, a dog at all things.

If I had not had more wit than he, to take a fault upon
me that he did, I think verily he had been hanged for't;
sure as I live, he had suffered for't. You shall judge. He
thrusts me himself into the company of three or four
gentlemanlike dogs under the Duke's table; he had not
been there, bless the mark, a pissing while but all the
chamber smelt him. 'Out with the dog!' says one;
'What cur is that?' says another; 'Whip him out,' says   20
the third; 'Hang him up,' says the Duke. I, having been
acquainted with the smell before, knew it was Crab, and
goes me to the fellow that whips the dogs. 'Friend,'
quoth I, 'you mean to whip the dog?' 'Ay, marry, do I,'
quoth he. 'You do him the more wrong,' quoth I,
''twas I did the thing you wot of.' He makes me no
more ado, but whips me out of the chamber. How many
masters would do this for his servant? Nay, I'll be
sworn, I have sat in the stocks for puddings he hath
stolen, otherwise he had been executed; I have stood on   30
the pillory for geese he hath killed, otherwise he had
suffered for't. Thou thinkest not of this now. Nay, I
remember the trick you served me when I took my leave
of Madam Silvia. Did not I bid thee still mark me and
do as I do? When didst thou see me heave up my leg
and make water against a gentlewoman's farthingale?
Didst thou ever see me do such a trick?

   Enter Proteus, and Julia in a page's costume

PROTEUS

Sebastian is thy name? I like thee well,
And will employ thee in some service presently.

JULIA

In what you please; I will do what I can.   40

PROTEUS

I hope thou wilt. (*To Launce*) How now, you whoreson
   peasant!

Where have you been these two days loitering?

LAUNCE Marry, sir, I carried Mistress Silvia the dog you bade me.

PROTEUS And what says she to my little jewel?

LAUNCE Marry, she says your dog was a cur, and tells you currish thanks is good enough for such a present.

PROTEUS But she received my dog?

LAUNCE No, indeed, did she not; here have I brought him back again.

50

PROTEUS What, didst thou offer her this from me?

LAUNCE Ay, sir; the other squirrel was stolen from me by the hangman boys in the market-place; and then I offered her mine own, who is a dog as big as ten of yours, and therefore the gift the greater.

PROTEUS

Go get thee hence and find my dog again,
Or ne'er return again into my sight.
Away, I say! Stayest thou to vex me here?

Exit Launce

A slave that still an end turns me to shame!
Sebastian, I have entertainèd thee,
Partly that I have need of such a youth
That can with some discretion do my business,
For 'tis no trusting to yond foolish lout;
But chiefly for thy face and thy behaviour,
Which, if my augury deceive me not,
Witness good bringing up, fortune, and truth;
Therefore, know thou, for this I entertain thee.
Go presently, and take this ring with thee,
Deliver it to Madam Silvia –

70

She loved me well delivered it to me.

JULIA

It seems you loved not her, to leave her token.
She is dead, belike?

60

PROTEUS   Not so; I think she lives.

JULIA
  Alas!

PROTEUS
  Why dost thou cry 'Alas'?

JULIA   I cannot choose
  But pity her.

PROTEUS   Wherefore shouldst thou pity her?

JULIA
  Because methinks that she loved you as well
  As you do love your lady Silvia.
  She dreams on him that has forgot her love;
  You dote on her that cares not for your love;
  'Tis pity love should be so contrary;   80
  And thinking on it makes me cry 'Alas!'

PROTEUS
  Well, give her that ring, and therewithal
  This letter. That's her chamber. Tell my lady
  I claim the promise for her heavenly picture.
  Your message done, hie home unto my chamber,
  Where thou shalt find me sad and solitary.   *Exit*

JULIA
  How many women would do such a message?
  Alas, poor Proteus, thou hast entertained
  A fox to be the shepherd of thy lambs.
  Alas, poor fool, why do I pity him   90
  That with his very heart despiseth me?
  Because he loves her, he despiseth me;
  Because I love him, I must pity him.
  This ring I gave him, when he parted from me,
  To bind him to remember my good will;
  And now am I, unhappy messenger,
  To plead for that which I would not obtain,
  To carry that which I would have refused,

To praise his faith, which I would have dispraised.
100 I am my master's true confirmèd love,
But cannot be true servant to my master,
Unless I prove false traitor to myself.
Yet will I woo for him, but yet so coldly
As, heaven it knows, I would not have him speed.
   Enter Silvia with Attendants
Gentlewoman, good day! I pray you, be my mean
To bring me where to speak with Madam Silvia.

SILVIA
What would you with her, if that I be she?

JULIA
If you be she, I do entreat your patience
To hear me speak the message I am sent on.

SILVIA
110 From whom?

JULIA
From my master, Sir Proteus, madam.

SILVIA
O, he sends you for a picture.

JULIA
Ay, madam.

SILVIA
Ursula, bring my picture there.
   *Exit one of the Attendants. She returns with a portrait
   of Silvia*
Go, give your master this. Tell him from me,
One Julia, that his changing thoughts forget,
Would better fit his chamber than this shadow.

JULIA
Madam, please you peruse this letter –
Pardon me, madam; I have unadvised
120 Delivered you a paper that I should not.

Julia takes back the letter she offers and gives Silvia
    another one

This is the letter to your ladyship.

SILVIA

I pray thee let me look on that again.

JULIA

It may not be; good madam, pardon me.

SILVIA

There, hold!

    She tears the letter

I will not look upon your master's lines.
I know they are stuffed with protestations,
And full of new-found oaths, which he will break
As easily as I do tear his paper.

JULIA

Madam, he sends your ladyship this ring.

SILVIA

The more shame for him that he sends it me;   130
For I have heard him say a thousand times
His Julia gave it him, at his departure.
Though his false finger have profaned the ring,
Mine shall not do his Julia so much wrong.

JULIA

She thanks you.

SILVIA

What sayest thou?

JULIA

I thank you, madam, that you tender her.
Poor gentlewoman! My master wrongs her much.

SILVIA

Dost thou know her?

JULIA

Almost as well as I do know myself.   140

To think upon her woes, I do protest
That I have wept a hundred several times.

SILVIA
Belike she thinks that Proteus hath forsook her.

JULIA
I think she doth, and that's her cause of sorrow.

SILVIA
Is she not passing fair?

JULIA
She hath been fairer, madam, than she is.
When she did think my master loved her well,
She, in my judgement, was as fair as you;
But since she did neglect her looking-glass
150   And threw her sun-expelling mask away,
That air hath starved the roses in her cheeks
And pinched the lily-tincture of her face,
That now she is become as black as I.

SILVIA
How tall was she?

JULIA
About my stature; for, at Pentecost,
When all our pageants of delight were played,
Our youth got me to play the woman's part
And I was trimmed in Madam Julia's gown,
Which servèd me as fit, by all men's judgements,
160   As if the garment had been made for me;
Therefore I know she is about my height.
And at that time I made her weep agood,
For I did play a lamentable part.
Madam, 'twas Ariadne passioning
For Theseus' perjury and unjust flight;
Which I so lively acted with my tears
That my poor mistress, movèd therewithal,
Wept bitterly; and would I might be dead

If I in thought felt not her very sorrow.

SILVIA

She is beholding to thee, gentle youth.   170
Alas, poor lady, desolate and left!
I weep myself, to think upon thy words.
Here, youth; there is my purse; I give thee this
For thy sweet mistress' sake, because thou lovest her.
Farewell.   *Exeunt Silvia and Attendants*

JULIA

And she shall thank you for't, if e'er you know her.
A virtuous gentlewoman, mild, and beautiful!
I hope my master's suit will be but cold,
Since she respects my mistress' love so much.
Alas, how love can trifle with itself!   180
Here is her picture; let me see. I think
If I had such a tire this face of mine
Were full as lovely as is this of hers;
And yet the painter flattered her a little,
Unless I flatter with myself too much.
Her hair is auburn, mine is perfect yellow;
If that be all the difference in his love,
I'll get me such a coloured periwig.
Her eyes are grey as glass, and so are mine;
Ay, but her forehead's low, and mine's as high.   190
What should it be that he respects in her
But I can make respective in myself,
If this fond Love were not a blinded god?
Come, shadow, come, and take this shadow up,
For 'tis thy rival. O, thou senseless form,
Thou shalt be worshipped, kissed, loved, and adored!
And were there sense in his idolatry,
My substance should be statue in thy stead.
I'll use thee kindly for thy mistress' sake,
That used me so; or else, by Jove I vow,   200

I should have scratched out your unseeing eyes,
To make my master out of love with thee!   *Exit*

*

V.1   *Enter Eglamour*

EGLAMOUR

The sun begins to gild the western sky,
And now it is about the very hour
That Silvia at Friar Patrick's cell should meet me.
She will not fail, for lovers break not hours
Unless it be to come before their time,
So much they spur their expedition.
        Enter Silvia
See where she comes. Lady, a happy evening!

SILVIA

Amen, amen! Go on, good Eglamour,
Out at the postern by the abbey wall;
10   I fear I am attended by some spies.

EGLAMOUR

Fear not. The forest is not three leagues off;
If we recover that, we are sure enough.   *Exeunt*

V.2   *Enter Thurio, Proteus, and Julia dressed in a page's
           costume*

THURIO

Sir Proteus, what says Silvia to my suit?

PROTEUS

O, sir, I find her milder than she was;
And yet she takes exceptions at your person.

THURIO

What? That my leg is too long?

PROTEUS

No, that it is too little.

THURIO

I'll wear a boot to make it somewhat rounder.

JULIA (*aside*)

But love will not be spurred to what it loathes.

THURIO

What says she to my face?

PROTEUS

She says it is a fair one.

THURIO

Nay then, the wanton lies; my face is black.   10

PROTEUS

But pearls are fair; and the old saying is:

Black men are pearls in beauteous ladies' eyes.

JULIA (*aside*)

'Tis true, such pearls as put out ladies' eyes;

For I had rather wink than look on them.

THURIO

How likes she my discourse?

PROTEUS

Ill, when you talk of war.

THURIO

But well when I discourse of love and peace.

JULIA (*aside*)

But better, indeed, when you hold your peace.

THURIO

What says she to my valour?

PROTEUS

O, sir, she makes no doubt of that.   20

JULIA (*aside*)

She needs not, when she knows it cowardice.

THURIO

What says she to my birth?

PROTEUS
     That you are well derived.
JULIA (*aside*)
     True; from a gentleman to a fool.
THURIO
     Considers she my possessions?
PROTEUS
     O, ay; and pities them.
THURIO
     Wherefore?
JULIA (*aside*)
     That such an ass should owe them.
PROTEUS
     That they are out by lease.
          Enter the Duke of Milan
JULIA
30   Here comes the Duke.
DUKE
     How now, Sir Proteus! How now, Thurio!
     Which of you saw Sir Eglamour of late?
THURIO
     Not I.
PROTEUS Nor I.
DUKE   Saw you my daughter?
PROTEUS   Neither.
DUKE
     Why then,
     She's fled unto that peasant Valentine;
     And Eglamour is in her company.
     'Tis true; for Friar Laurence met them both
     As he in penance wandered through the forest;
     Him he knew well, and guessed that it was she,
40   But, being masked, he was not sure of it;
     Besides, she did intend confession

At Patrick's cell this even; and there she was not.
These likelihoods confirm her flight from hence;
Therefore, I pray you, stand not to discourse,
But mount you presently, and meet with me
Upon the rising of the mountain-foot
That leads toward Mantua, whither they are fled.
Dispatch, sweet gentlemen, and follow me.   *Exit*

THURIO

Why, this it is to be a peevish girl
That flies her fortune when it follows her.
I'll after, more to be revenged on Eglamour   50
Than for the love of reckless Silvia.   *Exit*

PROTEUS

And I will follow, more for Silvia's love
Than hate of Eglamour, that goes with her.   *Exit*

JULIA

And I will follow, more to cross that love
Than hate for Silvia, that is gone for love.   *Exit*

Enter the Outlaws with Silvia captive   V.3

FIRST OUTLAW

Come, come,
Be patient; we must bring you to our captain.

SILVIA

A thousand more mischances than this one
Have learned me how to brook this patiently.

SECOND OUTLAW

Come, bring her away.

FIRST OUTLAW

Where is the gentleman that was with her?

THIRD OUTLAW

Being nimble-footed, he hath outrun us,
But Moyses and Valerius follow him.

Go thou with her to the west end of the wood;
10   There is our captain; we'll follow him that's fled.
The thicket is beset; he cannot 'scape.

FIRST OUTLAW

Come, I must bring you to our captain's cave;
Fear not; he bears an honourable mind,
And will not use a woman lawlessly.

SILVIA

O Valentine, this I endure for thee!   *Exeunt*

V.4   *Enter Valentine*

VALENTINE

How use doth breed a habit in a man!
This shadowy desert, unfrequented woods,
I better brook than flourishing peopled towns.
Here can I sit alone, unseen of any,
And to the nightingale's complaining notes
Tune my distresses, and record my woes.
O thou that dost inhabit in my breast,
Leave not the mansion so long tenantless,
Lest, growing ruinous, the building fall
10   And leave no memory of what it was!
Repair me with thy presence, Silvia;
Thou gentle nymph, cherish thy forlorn swain.
     Noises within
What halloing and what stir is this today?
These are my mates, that make their wills their law,
Have some unhappy passenger in chase.
They love me well; yet I have much to do
To keep them from uncivil outrages.
Withdraw thee, Valentine. Who's this comes here?
     He steps aside
     Enter Proteus, Silvia, and Julia in a page's costume

PROTEUS

Madam, this service I have done for you,
Though you respect not aught your servant doth,   20
To hazard life, and rescue you from him
That would have forced your honour and your love.
Vouchsafe me, for my meed, but one fair look;
A smaller boon than this I cannot beg,
And less than this, I am sure, you cannot give.

VALENTINE (*aside*)

How like a dream is this I see and hear!
Love, lend me patience to forbear awhile.

SILVIA

O miserable, unhappy that I am!

PROTEUS

Unhappy were you, madam, ere I came;
But by my coming I have made you happy.   30

SILVIA

By thy approach thou makest me most unhappy.

JULIA (*aside*)

And me, when he approacheth to your presence.

SILVIA

Had I been seizèd by a hungry lion,
I would have been a breakfast to the beast,
Rather than have false Proteus rescue me.
O, heaven be judge how I love Valentine,
Whose life's as tender to me as my soul!
And full as much, for more there cannot be,
I do detest false perjured Proteus.
Therefore be gone; solicit me no more.   40

PROTEUS

What dangerous action, stood it next to death,
Would I not undergo for one calm look?
O, 'tis the curse in love, and still approved,
When women cannot love where they're beloved!

SILVIA

    When Proteus cannot love where he's beloved!
    Read over Julia's heart, thy first best love,
    For whose dear sake thou didst then rend thy faith
    Into a thousand oaths; and all those oaths
    Descended into perjury, to love me.
50   Thou hast no faith left now, unless thou'dst two,
    And that's far worse than none; better have none
    Than plural faith, which is too much by one.
    Thou counterfeit to thy true friend!

PROTEUS   In love,

    Who respects friend?

SILVIA   All men but Proteus.

PROTEUS

    Nay, if the gentle spirit of moving words
    Can no way change you to a milder form,
    I'll woo you like a soldier, at arms' end,
    And love you 'gainst the nature of love – force ye.

SILVIA

    O heaven!

PROTEUS   I'll force thee yield to my desire.

    Valentine steps forward

VALENTINE

60   Ruffian, let go that rude uncivil touch;
    Thou friend of an ill fashion!

PROTEUS   Valentine!

VALENTINE

    Thou common friend that's without faith or love –
    For such is a friend now; treacherous man,
    Thou hast beguiled my hopes; naught but mine eye
    Could have persuaded me. Now I dare not say
    I have one friend alive: thou wouldst disprove me.
    Who should be trusted now, when one's right hand
    Is perjured to the bosom? Proteus,

I am sorry I must never trust thee more,
But count the world a stranger for thy sake.   70
The private wound is deepest. O time most accurst!
'Mongst all foes that a friend should be the worst!

PROTEUS
My shame and guilt confounds me.
Forgive me, Valentine; if hearty sorrow
Be a sufficient ransom for offence,
I tender't here; I do as truly suffer
As e'er I did commit.

VALENTINE   Then I am paid;
And once again I do receive thee honest.
Who by repentance is not satisfied
Is nor of heaven nor earth, for these are pleased;   80
By penitence th'Eternal's wrath's appeased.
And, that my love may appear plain and free,
All that was mine in Silvia I give thee.

JULIA O me unhappy!
      She swoons

PROTEUS Look to the boy.

VALENTINE Why, boy? Why, wag, how now? What's the
    matter? Look up; speak.

JULIA O, good sir, my master charged me to deliver a ring
    to Madam Silvia, which, out of my neglect, was never
    done.   90

PROTEUS Where is that ring, boy?

JULIA Here 'tis; this is it.
      She offers her own ring

PROTEUS How? Let me see. Why, this is the ring I gave
    to Julia.

JULIA
O, cry you mercy, sir, I have mistook;
This is the ring you sent to Silvia.
      She offers another ring

PROTEUS But how camest thou by this ring? At my depart
    I gave this unto Julia.

JULIA
    And Julia herself did give it me;
100   And Julia herself hath brought it hither.

PROTEUS
    How? Julia?

JULIA
    Behold her that gave aim to all thy oaths,
    And entertained 'em deeply in her heart.
    How oft hast thou with perjury cleft the root!
    O Proteus, let this habit make thee blush!
    Be thou ashamed that I have took upon me
    Such an immodest raiment, if shame live
    In a disguise of love.
    It is the lesser blot, modesty finds,
110   Women to change their shapes than men their minds.

PROTEUS
    Than men their minds? 'Tis true. O heaven, were man
    But constant, he were perfect! That one error
    Fills him with faults; makes him run through all the
        sins:
    Inconstancy falls off ere it begins.
    What is in Silvia's face, but I may spy
    More fresh in Julia's with a constant eye?

VALENTINE
    Come, come, a hand from either.
    Let me be blest to make this happy close;
    'Twere pity two such friends should be long foes.

PROTEUS
120   Bear witness, heaven, I have my wish for ever.

JULIA
    And I mine.

Enter the Outlaws, with the Duke of Milan and Thurio
captives

OUTLAWS

A prize, a prize, a prize!

VALENTINE   Forbear,

Forbear, I say! It is my lord the Duke.

Your grace is welcome to a man disgraced,

Banishèd Valentine.

DUKE   Sir Valentine?

THURIO

Yonder is Silvia; and Silvia's mine.

VALENTINE

Thurio, give back, or else embrace thy death;

Come not within the measure of my wrath;

Do not name Silvia thine; if once again,

Verona shall not hold thee. Here she stands;   130

Take but possession of her with a touch –

I dare thee but to breathe upon my love.

THURIO

Sir Valentine, I care not for her, I:

I hold him but a fool that will endanger

His body for a girl that loves him not.

I claim her not and therefore she is thine.

DUKE

The more degenerate and base art thou

To make such means for her as thou hast done,

And leave her on such slight conditions.

Now, by the honour of my ancestry,   140

I do applaud thy spirit, Valentine,

And think thee worthy of an empress' love.

Know, then, I here forget all former griefs,

Cancel all grudge, repeal thee home again,

Plead a new state in thy unrivalled merit,

To which I thus subscribe: Sir Valentine.
Thou art a gentleman, and well derived;
Take thou thy Silvia, for thou hast deserved her.

VALENTINE

I thank your grace; the gift hath made me happy.
150 I now beseech you, for your daughter's sake,
To grant one boon that I shall ask of you.

DUKE

I grant it, for thine own, whate'er it be.

VALENTINE

These banished men, that I have kept withal,
Are men endued with worthy qualities;
Forgive them what they have committed here,
And let them be recalled from their exile:
They are reformèd, civil, full of good,
And fit for great employment, worthy lord.

DUKE

Thou hast prevailed; I pardon them and thee;
160 Dispose of them as thou knowest their deserts.
Come, let us go; we will include all jars
With triumphs, mirth, and rare solemnity.

VALENTINE

And, as we walk along, I dare be bold
With our discourse to make your grace to smile.
What think you of this page, my lord?

DUKE

I think the boy hath grace in him; he blushes.

VALENTINE

I warrant you, my lord – more grace than boy.

DUKE

What mean you by that saying?

VALENTINE

Please you, I'll tell you as we pass along,
170 That you will wonder what hath fortunèd.

Come, Proteus, 'tis your penance but to hear
The story of your loves discoverèd.
That done, our day of marriage shall be yours:
One feast, one house, one mutual happiness. *Exeunt*

An Account of the Text

The Two Gentlemen of Verona was first published in the Folio of 1623 in which it is the second play in the volume. A collation of the bulk of the extant copies of the Folio indicates that some pages of the play were subjected to careful proofreading and correction during the printing, for the details of which see the first list of collations. This text is the only one which has any authority; the texts found in the later Folios of 1632, 1664 and 1685 make some obvious corrections but are all ultimately based on the first printing.

The Folio text has certain unusual features shared by only one other play in the volume, *The Merry Wives of Windsor*. First, apart from the endings of the scenes, the marking of characters' exits is notably absent, only four (those at I.1.62, I.2.49, II.1.127 and II.4.189) being signalled. Secondly, all entrances are bunched at the heads of the scenes; for example, the Folio stage direction at the beginning of V.4 reads '*Enter Valentine, Protheus, Siluia, Iulia, Duke, Thurio, Out-lawes.*', although only Valentine enters initially; Proteus, Julia and Silvia do not enter until line 18, and the Outlaws, the Duke and Thurio until line 121. These characteristics together with the Folio's lavish use of hyphens and parentheses have been seen to suggest that the text was set up from a manuscript prepared for the press by Ralph Crane, the scrivener of the King's Men's Company, whose copying work possessed these idiosyncrasies, and who also prepared manuscripts of *The Tempest*, *The Merry Wives of Windsor* and *Measure for Measure* for the printers of the Folio.

While it can be argued with some confidence that the Folio text was set up from a transcript rather than from a playhouse manuscript (which obviously could not have exhibited such features), it is far more difficult to determine with any accuracy what sort of copy was the basis of Crane's work. One theory, developed by J. Dover Wilson, accounts for some though not all of the text's characteristics. Wilson claims that the manuscript was a composite or 'assembled' text made up from the individual actors' 'parts' with the aid of a 'platte' or outline of the action which was hung in the theatre for the company's use and gave the scenes of the play, together with the names of the actors, in order of appearance, playing in each one. Attractive as the theory is, however, most scholars have viewed it with some scepticism, noting that the text appears to be noticeably free from the kind of errors one would expect in such a process – for example, the false sequence of speeches or the accidental inclusion of cues in the lines following them.

Because of the shortness of the play (some 2,600 lines), the unsatisfactory nature of certain scenes and the weakness of parts of the verse, most scholars have been convinced that the Folio text is based ultimately on a shortened version of Shakespeare's original play – adapted perhaps for a small travelling company of players – a practice common at the time and one to which some of Shakespeare's other plays appear to have been subjected.

The pieces of evidence adduced for this truncation are complex in nature but some of the most striking may be given here:

(1) There are passages which seem to be the result of unskilful 'cutting' or need emendation to produce sense; for example, II.4.194–6, III.2.75–81 and V.4.55–8.

(2) Isolated prose passages appear in the middle of verse scenes and, conversely, snippets of verse appear in prose passages; for example V.4.84–98.

(3) There are scenes (for example, II.2 and V.3) which seem to be curtailed. These may be the conclusions of longer scenes, the suppression of which the adapter has attempted to conceal by writing a few lines of prose as an introduction.

(4) Passages occur in which the sense is clear but which are at odds with what has taken place on the stage. For example, at the end of II.4 Proteus in soliloquy says:

'Tis but her picture I have yet beheld,
And that hath dazzlèd my reason's light;
But when I look on her perfections,
There is no reason but I shall be blind. (207–10)

Yet, this immediately follows his conversation with Valentine and
Silvia over a space of seventeen lines (97–113). This contradic-
tion, taken together with the use made of Silvia's portrait at
IV.2.117–29 and IV.4.83–4, 112–17, 181–202, may suggest that
there was originally a scene preceding II.4 in which Valentine
showed Proteus a portrait of Silvia, with which he became
infatuated.

(5) The time-sequence of the play is confused; for example,
some scholars have suggested that a break is necessary at III.1.187
and that an interval is needed between IV.3 and IV.4.

(6) The use of names is sometimes inconsistent; for example,
the Duke of Milan is referred to sometimes as a duke and sometimes as an emperor, and Antonio's servant appears on some occa-
sions as 'Panthino' and on others as 'Panthion'.

(7) The location of scenes is not always clear; for example, at
II.5.1 Speed, in Milan, welcomes Launce to Padua; at III.1.81 the
Duke of Milan speaks of 'a lady in Verona here' (F); and at
V.4.130 Valentine addresses Thurio, a Milanese, as if he were a
citizen of Verona.

(8) The final scene contains a number of puzzling and unsatisfactory features such as Proteus's unbelievably rapid repentance, Valentine's ready acceptance of it and offer of Silvia to his
friend, and Silvia's unnatural silence for some 115 lines.

In conclusion, while there is no general agreement either on
the various solutions offered to explain the above difficulties or
on the nature of the manuscript which was the source of the Folio
text, it is fair to say that most scholars believe that what we have
is an imperfect and probably shortened version of Shakespeare's
play, but one which was sufficiently close to the original to have
persuaded John Heminges and Henry Condell, Shakespeare's
fellow-actors and the editors of the Folio, to include it in their
collection as the poet's work.

COLLATIONS

The following lists are *selective*. They include the more important and interesting variants. Minor changes which are not
disputed, small variations in word order, mislineation, obvious
misprints and grammatical corrections not affecting the sense are
not usually included here.

l

Below are listed departures in the present text of *The Two
Gentlemen of Verona* from that of the Folio (F), whose readings
are given on the right of the square bracket. Most of these altera-
tions were first made by eighteenth-century editors of the play.
Some of these departures were made in one of the seventeenth-
century reprints of the Folio (F2, F3, and F4) and are so indicated.

I.I

      12 haply] (hap'ly)
      43 dwells,] dwels;
      65 leave] loue
      75 An] And
      77 I a sheep] (F2); I Sheepe
  110–13 PROTEUS But what said she? | *Speed nods* | A nod?
          | SPEED Ay. | PROTEUS Nod-ay? Why, that's
          noddy.] *Pro*. But what said she? | *Sp*.I. | *Pro*. Nod-I,
          why that's noddy.
     140 What said she? Nothing?] What said she, nothing?
     142 testerned] (F2); cestern'd

I.2

      83 'Light o'love'] *Light O, Loue*
      96 your] (F2); you

I.3

      24 whither] whether
      88 father calls] Fathers call's

II.I

      19 malcontent] Male-content
      93 give] 'giue

108 Please you command, a] (Please you command) a

II.2

19 I come] I come, I come

II.3

26 an old woman] a would-woman

35, 36,
38, 49 tied] tide
36 tied] Tide
47 my] thy

II.4

11 Haply] Hap'ly
34 madam. We] Madam, we
59 know] knew
91 Nay, then,] Nay then
106 worthy mistress) (F2); worthy a Mistresse
114 SERVANT] *Thur.*
155 too] to
164 makes] make
172–3 likes | Only for his possessions are so huge,]
        likes | (Onely . . . huge)
175 love, thou knowest, is full of jealousy.] Loue (thou
        know'st is full of iealousie.)
194 Is it mine eye, or] It is mine, or

II.5

1 Milan] *Padua*
37 thou that] (F2); thou that that
46 wilt, go] wilt goe

II.6

1, 2 forsworn;] forsworne?

II.7

37 rest as,] rest, as
        turmoil,] turmoile
67 withal] (F2); with all

III.1

81 lady of Verona] Lady in *Verona*
173 self – a] selfe. A
271 *Imprimis] Inprimis*
278 master's ship] Mastership
291 try] *some copies of* F *have* thy

293 *Imprimis*] Inprimi
313 follow] *some copies of* F *have* followes
315 *be kissed fasting*] be fasting
323 talk] *some copies of* F *have* take
346 last] *some copies of* F *have this word omitted*

III.2

14 grievously] *some copies of* F *have* heauily

IV.1

10 he's] he is
33 travel] trauaile
34 been miserable] beene often miserable
49 An heir, and near allied] And heire and Neece, alide

IV.2

110 his] her

IV.3

17 abhors] abhor'd
40 Recking] Wreaking

IV.4

 5 precisely, 'Thus] precisely, thus
45 jewel] Iewell
53 hangman boys] Hangmans boyes
67 know thou] know thee
71 to leave] not leaue
186 auburn] *Aburne*

V.2

 7 JULIA] *Prot.*
13 JULIA] *Thu.*
18 your] you
32 saw Sir Eglamour] (F4); saw *Eglamoure*

V.4

 6 distresses] distrestes
26 this I] this? I
67 trusted now, when] (F2); trusted, when

2

The following list records a selection of emendations which have
not been adopted in the present edition, but which have either
been made with some plausibility in Folios 2, 3 and 4, or been

made and conjectured in other editions of the play. To the left of
the square brackets are the readings of the present text, and to
the right of them the Folio reading when it differs from that of
the present text and the suggested emendations.

I.I

    8 with] in
  19 my] thy
  25 for] but; and
  30 fading] *omitted*
  48 blasting] blasted
  57 To Milan] To Milan!; At Milan
  67 Made] Make
  99 such store] such a store
 103 astray] a stray
 107 a] the
110–13 PROTEUS But what said she? | *Speed nods* | A nod?
    | SPEED Ay. | PROTEUS Nod-ay? Why, that's
    noddy.] (F: *Pro.* But what said she? | *Sp. I. Pro.*
    Nod-I, why that's noddy.); *Pro.* But what said she? |
    Sp. (*nodding*) Ay. | *Pro.* Nod ay? why, that's noddy;
    Pro. But what said she? | *Speed nods, Proteus looks at*
    Speed in question | *Sp.* Ay. | *Pro.* Why, that's noddy.
114, 115 say] said
 122 orderly] motherly; elderly; elder-like
 129 at once] *omitted*
 133 Why?] Why,
 135 her;] her better;
 137 brought your] brought her; brought you her
 140 What said she? Nothing?] (F: What said she,
    nothing?); What, said she nothing?

I.2

  1 now we are] now are we
  8 shallow simple] shallow-simple
 10 of a knight] our knight
 12 Mercatio] Mercutio
 15 reigns] feigns
 18 am] can
 19 thus] pass
    on lovely] on a lovely; on this lovely; on a loving

28 loves] loved
80 tune] time
97 bid] bide; did
121 fearful, hanging] fearful-hanging

I.3

21 and] nor
32 in eye] in the eye
49 To] And
65 there] there's
67 Valentinus] Valentino; Valentine
73 Please you] Please to
84 resembleth] resembleth well; resembleth right;
resembleth soon
86 sun] light
91 it answers] (F: it answer's); its answer's

II.1

22 buried] lost
28–9 are metamorphosed] are so metamorphosed
37 you like] you; like
73 to put on your hose] to put on your shoes; to put on
your clothes; beyond your nose; to put spectacles
on your nose
108 Please you command, a] (F: (Please you command)
a); Please you command a
152 there] there's

II.3

21 I am the dog] I am me
21–2 O, the dog is me] Ay, the dog is the dog
26 she] the shoe
now] more
an old woman] (F: a would-woman); a wood
woman; an ould woman; a wold-woman; a wild
woman

II.4

54 worth] wealth
80 he] this
83 cite] 'cite (= incite)
97 gentleman.] gentleman. *Exit Thurio*
99 his] this

113 *Enter a Servant*] *Re-enter Thurio*
128 Whose] Those
    high imperious] high-imperious
    thoughts] thongs
135 as I confess] as, I confess,
137 no such] any
146 praises] praise
160 summer-swelling] summer-smelling
164 worthies] worth as
194 Is it mine eye, or Valentine's praise] (F: It is mine,
    or *Valentines* praise); Is it mine then, or Valentineans
    praise; Is it mine then or Valentino's praise; Is it
    mine eyne, or Valentino's praise; Is it mine own, or
    Valentino's praise; Is it her mien, or Valentinus'
    praise; Is it mine eye, or Valentinus' praise; Is it my
    mind, or Valentinus' praise; Is it or mine, or
    Valentine's praise; Is it mine unstaid mind, or
    Valentine's praise
208 light] sight

II.6

  7 sweet-suggesting] sweet suggestion,
    if thou hast] if I have
 21 thus] this
    by] but
 24 in] to
 37 pretended] intended

II.7

 18 inly] inchly
 24 dammest] damp'st
 32 wild] wide; mild
 70 of infinite] as infinite; of the infinite; o' the infinite
 85 longing] loving
 89 to] do

III.1

 21 unprevented] unprepared
 81 lady of Verona] (F: Lady in *Verona*); lady in Milan;
    lady in Milano; lady, sir, in Milan
149 *should* would
173 self – a] (F: selfe. A); self: ah,; self. Ah!

185 his] this; is
240 As] An
anthem] Amen
263 one knave] one kind of knave; one kind; one in love
271 cate-log] catalogue; cat-log
293 *Imprimis*] (F: Inprimi); *Item*
313 Here follow her vices] 'Here follow her vices'
322 sleep] slip
325 villain] villany
343 *hair*] hairs
346 that last] that
349 be I'll] be; I'll

III.2

14 grievously] heavily
19 better] bolder
21 grace] face
49 weed] wend; wind; wean; woo
55 worth] word
64 Where] When
76 line] lines
77 such] strict; love's
integrity] idolatry
84 consort] concert

IV.1

4 sit] sir
11 wealth] left
46 awful] lawful
49 An heir, and near allied] (F: And heire and Neece,
alide); An heir, and niece allied
52 such like] such-like
63 this] the
74 crews] crew; cave; caves; cruives
76 all] shall

IV.2

5 fair] pure
25 tune] turn
72 I tell] I will tell
90 even] ever

113 hers] her

IV.3

  38 placed] caused

IV.4

   5 say precisely, 'Thus] (F: say precisely, thus), say, 'Precisely

 34 Silvia] Julia

 45 jewel] (F: Iewell); Jewel

 52 other squirrel] other, Squirrel

 53 hangman boys] (F: Hangmans boyes); Hangman's boys

 67 know thou] (F: know thee); know that

 71 to leave] (F: not leaue); not love; nor love

127 new-found] new coined

152 pinched] pitched; pinced

179 my] his

189 grey as glass] green as grass

198 statue] statued; sainted; statua; shadow

V.2

 17 peace.] peace?

 32 you saw Sir Eglamour] (F: you saw *Eglamoure*); you say you saw Sir Eglamour

V.3

  8 Moyses] Moses

V.4

  2 This shadowy desert] These shadowy, desert

 47 rend thy] rent thy; candy

 49 Descended] Re-rented; Discandied
perjury,] perjury.
love] deceive

 57 woo] move

 63 treacherous] though treacherous

 67 trusted now, when one's right] (F: trusted, when ones right); trusted, when one's own right

 71 time most accurst] time most curst; time accurst

 83 mine] thine
I give] I'd give; I 'give (= forgive)

114 Inconstancy] In constancy

130 Verona shall not hold thee] Milan shall not behold
    thee; Milan shall not hold thee; Milan e'en shall not
    hold thee; Milano shall not hold thee; Verona shall
    not hold me
145 Plead] Plant
    state] statute
    unrivalled] arrivalled
161 include] conclude
162 rare] all

3

In the Folio text, for the majority of the scenes, the opening stage
direction indicates the entry of all the characters who appear in
the scene at any point, and there is some final indication of clearing
the stage. Within the scenes there are no indications of entry of
characters at appropriate points, and there are only four examples of marked exits (at I.1.62, I.2.49, II.1.127, II.4.189). In the
present edition, the stage directions at the opening of scenes have
been corrected and the Folio's exits have been retained. All other
stage directions (entrances and exits within the scenes and indications of stage action) have been supplied by the present editor.

4

The following list of characters appears at the end of the text in
the Folio. There is no general agreement about who composed it.

The names of all the Actors.

Duke: Father to Siluia.
Valentine. ⎫
        ⎬ *the two Gentlemen.*
Protheus. ⎭
Anthonio: father to Protheus.
Thurio: a foolish riuall to Valentine.
Eglamoure: Agent for Siluia in her escape.
Host: where Iulia lodges.
Out-lawes with Valentine.
Speed: a clownish seruant to Valentine.

Launce: the like to Protheus.
Panthion: seruant to Antonio.
Iulia: beloued of Protheus.
Siluia: beloued of Valentine.
Lucetta: waighting-woman to Iulia.

Commentary

The act and scene divisions are those of the Folio (F). Passages from Jorge de Montemayor's *La Diana* (translated by B. Yong in 1598) are modern-spelling versions of the text, found, under the title 'The Story of Felix and Felismena', in *Elizabethan Love Stories*, edited by T. J. B. Spencer (1968); those from Sir Thomas Elyot's *Book of the Governor* (1531) are modern-spelling versions of the text, found in *Narrative and Dramatic Sources of Shakespeare*, edited by G. Bullough, Vol. I (1957); page references are given to these sources. Quotations from the works of John Lyly are modern-spelling versions of the text, found in R. W. Bond's edition of *The Complete Works of John Lyly* (1902), to which references are given.

I.I

   o *Valentine*: By association with the St Valentine's Day tradition the word means 'a true lover'. See Launce's and Valentine's quibbles on the name at III.1.191–214.
       Proteus: The name is spelt *Protheus* throughout F. In Greek mythology Proteus was an old man of the sea who guarded the flocks of Poseidon. Although he had the gift of prophecy, those who wished to consult him found that on being questioned he eluded them by assuming different shapes.

   2 *Home-keeping youth have ever homely wits*: Among the upper classes of Shakespeare's day travelling was beginning to be considered an educational and broadening experience appropriate for a young man. Cf. Lucentio's attitude in *The Taming of the Shrew* (I.1.1–24) and Petruchio's conversation with Hortensio at

I.2.47–51 in the same play:

HORTENSIO
    And tell me now, sweet friend, what happy gale
    Blows you to Padua here from old Verona?
PETRUCHIO
    Such wind as scatters young men through the world
    To seek their fortunes farther than at home,
    Where small experience grows.

3   *affection*: Passion, love.
8   *shapeless*: Aimless, without guidance or direction.
9   *still*: Always, constantly.
12–13   *Think on thy Proteus . . . in thy travel*: Ironical in view
        of the fact that Silvia is to be the most *rare noteworthy
        object* that Valentine is to meet in Milan.
12   *haply*: By chance.
15   *hap*: Fortune.
18   *beadsman*: A holy man engaged to pray (that is, tell the
        beads of his rosary) for another person.
19   *love-book*: Manual of courtship or a romance, instead
        of a prayer-book.
21   *shallow story of deep love*: The quibble here is on *shallow*
        and *deep* water and *shallow* (not profound) and *deep*
        (passionate) love.
22   *How young Leander crossed the Hellespont*: The refer-
        ence is to the legend of Leander who swam the
        Hellespont each night to visit his mistress, Hero. It may
        also be an allusion to Christopher Marlowe's poem *Hero
        and Leander*, which was entered for publication in the
        Register of the Stationers' Company in 1593, after
        Marlowe's death, but was not printed until 1598.
23   *deep story of a deeper love*: The quibble is on *deep*
        (meaning 'profound', 'tragic') and *deeper* (meaning
        'farther in the depths of the sea'), the allusion being to
        Leander's ultimate death by drowning as he crossed
        the Hellespont in rough weather.
24   *over-shoes in love*: Determined recklessly to pursue his
        love affair. The quibble is with *over-shoes* (meaning

'wet above the shoes') as Leander was in the Hellespont.

25 *over-boots*: The same as *over-shoes*; see note to 24.

27 *give me not the boots*: A proverbial expression meaning 'do not make a fool of me, do not play with me'.

28 *it boots thee not*: It avails you not. The quibble is with the proverbial phrase at 27.

29–35 *To be in love, where scorn is bought with groans . . . vanquishèd*: This passage is made up of Renaissance commonplaces about romantic love and contains most of the conventional attitudes attributed to the lover at this period. Cf. Speed's satirical picture of the lover at II.1.17–30. More specifically the tone of the passage, as well as the play's opposition between love and friendship, recalls John Lyly's *Euphues, The Anatomy of Wit*, an enormously popular and influential novel published in 1578.

32–3 *If haply won . . . a grievous labour won*: These lines are sometimes taken as an allusion to Shakespeare's play *Love's Labour's Lost* and to the play *Love's Labour's Won*, which is not extant but which is listed as being by Shakespeare in Francis Meres's *Palladis Tamia* (1598).

32 *hapless*: Unfortunate.

34 *However*: In any case, however it may turn out.

34–5 *a folly bought with wit . . . a wit by folly vanquishèd*: An Elizabethan commonplace; cf. *As You Like It* (II.7.182): 'Most friendship is feigning, most loving mere folly . . .'

34 *wit*: Intellect, mind.

36 *circumstance*: Peroration, argument, detailed discourse.

37 *circumstance*: Situation, condition.

41 *chronicled for wise*: Literally this means 'set down in the Chronicle for wisdom', but here it merely means 'reputed to be wise'.

43 *canker*: Cankerworm.

44 *Inhabits in*: Dwells in.
   wits: Minds, intellects.

45 *forward*: Advanced in growth.

46 *blow*: Bloom, blossom.

49 *his verdure*: Its fresh or flourishing condition.
   prime: Spring.

50 *fair effects of future hopes*: Prosperous fulfilment of
   future happiness.

52 *votary to*: Addicted to, with the religious overtone
   implying 'worshipping'.
   fond: Doting, and thus 'foolish'.

53 *road*: Harbour, anchorage.

54 *shipped*: Both Valentine here and Proteus (at II.2.14 and
   II.4.185) go by sea from Verona to Milan; whereas Julia
   makes the journey overland (see II.7.8–10, 35), as does
   Valentine on his return journey. One of the features of
   F is the confusion in place names and locations; see An
   Account of the Text.

55 *bring*: Accompany.

57 *To Milan*: Although some editors emend with F2 to *At
   Milan*, the syntax is not unusual and means 'by letters
   (sent) to Milan'.

58 *success*: Fortune (good or bad).

59 *Betideth*: Takes place.

61 *bechance*: Befall.

65 *leave*: F's *love* makes no sense here and is probably a
   compositor's misreading of 'loue' for 'leue'.

66–9 *Thou, Julia . . . hast metamorphosed me . . . with thought*:
   Proteus describes here all the symptoms generally
   ascribed to the young lover during the Elizabethan
   period; cf. *Romeo and Juliet*, I.1.171–237.

66 *metamorphosed*: The first reference in the play to the
   traditional Protean nature.

67 *lose*: Waste.

69 *thought*: Brooding melancholy.

70 *save you*: God save you, a common greeting of the
   time.

73 *sheep*: A quibble on 'ship' (from *shipped* at 72), the two
   words being apparently pronounced sufficiently alike
   at the time. Cf. the similar use in *The Comedy of Errors*
   (IV.1.94–5) and *Love's Labour's Lost* (II.1.205–8).

75 *An*: If. 'An if' was a frequently used double form.

79 *my horns are his horns*: It has been suggested that the

reference here is to the rhyme 'Little Boy Blue'; but it
is possibly a pointless allusion to the horns of the
cuckold.

84 *circumstance*: Detailed proof or argument.

93 *'baa'*: The quibble is with 'bah!'.

94–5 *Gavest thou my letter to Julia*: There is no reason why
      Proteus should employ Valentine's servant rather than
      Launce, except possibly for secrecy in his affair which
      at I.3.51–9 he seems intent on keeping from his father's
      knowledge. In *La Diana*, Don Felix (Proteus) also
      makes his first approach to his mistress by means of a
      letter which is conveyed to Felismena (Julia) by her
      maid Rosina (Lucetta); see *Elizabethan Love Stories*, pp.
      132–3.

96–7 *I, a lost mutton, gave your letter to her, a laced mutton*:
      It is clear, however, from the exchange between Julia
      and Lucetta at I.2.34 ff. that Speed did not meet Julia,
      so that here he has been talking about the maid's rather
      than the mistress's behaviour.

97 *laced mutton*: A cant term for a prostitute, with *laced*
    referring either to the lace or slashing of her dress
    or to her tight lacing. Speed pronounced *laced* suffi-
    ciently like *lost* to pun with his phrase at 96. The way
    in which Proteus accepts this impertinence has caused
    many editors to suspect that this exchange is an
    interpolation. However, there is ample evidence in
    Shakespeare's other plays to indicate that the relation-
    ship between young men and their servants was a good
    deal more flexible than class-conscious nineteenth-
    century commentators were prepared to allow. Good-
    humoured familiarity between the young master
    and his servant was also a feature of the Roman come-
    dies of Plautus and Terence, which Shakespeare knew
    well.

101 *overcharged*: Overburdened, overstocked (with sheep).
     you were best: It would be best for you.
     stick: Stab, slaughter (the excessive sheep). Speed almost
     certainly means to suggest a bawdy quibble (the mutton
     meaning the prostitute).

103 *astray*: Proteus is echoing Speed's phrase *I, a lost mutton* and quibbles 'a stray'.

   pound: The quibble is on the two meanings 'enclose' (like a stray sheep) and 'beat'.

105 *pound*: Speed deliberately misunderstands Proteus, and assumes he is referring to the sum of money Speed will be paid for the errand.

107 *pinfold*: Enclosure for stray animals.

108–9 *From a pound to a pin? . . . carrying a letter to your lover*: F prints these lines as rhyming doggerel; and they could be delivered as bad impromptu verse in the theatre.

108 *a pin*: Something of no value.

110–13 *But what said she . . . that's noddy*: Most editors have felt it necessary to emend the F version of this passage so as to make the action conform to Speed's description at 114–15. See the second list of collations for other emendations which have been suggested.

113 *noddy*: Simpleton.

120 *fain*: Pleased.

   bear with you: The quibble is on 'endure' and 'support'.

122 *Marry*: This was a common exclamation meaning originally 'by the Virgin Mary'.

   nothing: The pun is with 'nodding' (through previous use of *nod* and *noddy*).

124 *Beshrew me*: A mild oath used for emphasis.

126 *open*: Disclose.

129 *delivered*: Speed is playing on '(the money) handed over' and '(the account) reported'.

133 *perceive*: Receive.

136 *ducat*: A gold or silver coin.

138 *in telling your mind*: When you tell her in person.

139 *stones*: The reference may be to diamonds which would be a suitable gift for someone with a hard nature.

142 *testerned*: Tipped with a tester (or sixpence). This coin was worth about one seventh of the ducat that Speed mentions hopefully at 136.

147 *destined to a drier death on shore*: The reference is to the proverb 'He that is born to be hanged shall never be drowned'.

149–50 *I fear my Julia would not deign my lines . . . from such
a worthless post*: This emphasis on appearance is characteristic of Proteus's way of thinking and quite
different from Julia's.

149 *deign*: Condescend to accept, take graciously.

150 *post*: The two meanings suggested are 'messenger' and
'door-post' (that is, blockhead).

I.2

1–33 *But say, Lucetta, now we are alone . . . his mind*:
Shakespeare was to use this situation with greater wit
in *The Merchant of Venice*, I.2, where Portia and Nerissa
discuss the suitors at Belmont. In *La Diana* Felismena
(Julia) relates how her maid Rosina (Lucetta) delivered the letter to her:

> But to see the means that Rosina made unto me . . . the
> dutiful services and unwonted circumstances before she
> did deliver it, the oaths that she sware unto me, and the
> subtle words and serious protestations she used, it was a
> pleasant thing and worthy the noting. (*Elizabethan Love
> Stories*, p. 133)

4 *resort*: Company, gathering.

5 *parle*: Talk, conversation.

6 *worthiest love*: Most worthy of love.

7 *show my mind*: Give you a description of them as I see
them.

9 *Sir Eglamour*: The name appears to have been a type
name for a carpet-knight. This is presumably a different
character from the Eglamour who accompanies Silvia
on her flight in V.1, although her description in
IV.3.11–13 is similar to Lucetta's here. The fact that
the same name is used twice is another sign of the care-
lessness which characterizes the text.

10 *neat*: Refined, elegant.

12 *Mercatio*: Some editors emend this to the commoner
Italian form 'Mercutio' that Shakespeare uses in *Romeo
and Juliet*.

17 *passing*: Surpassing.

19 *censure*: Pass judgement.

27 *moved me*: Approached me on the subject, made a proposal to me.

30 *Fire that's closest kept burns most of all*: An Elizabethan proverb.

Fire: Pronounced with two syllables here.

33–40 *I would I knew his mind . . . I pray*: The change in the metre occurs at the point where the subject of the letter is introduced. Some editors think Shakespeare intended line 38 to be a continuation of the three-stress pattern and print it as two lines.

41–7 *Now, by my modesty, a goodly broker . . . my sight*: In *La Diana* Felismena (Julia) also describes how she feigns annoyance with Rosina (Lucetta) on the delivery of the letter:

> To whom, nevertheless, with an angry countenance I turned again, saying: 'If I had not regard of mine own estate and what hereafter might be said, I would make this shameless face of thine be known ever after for a mark of an impudent and bold minion. But because it is the first time, let this suffice that I have said and give thee warning to take heed of the second.' (*Elizabethan Love Stories*, p. 133)

41 *broker*: Pandar, go-between.

50–65 *And yet I would I had o'erlooked the letter . . . folly past*: The episode in *La Diana* is quite close to these lines:

> And with this . . . taking her letter with her, she departed from me. This having passed thus, I began to imagine what might ensue thereof. And love, methought, did put a certain desire into my mind to see the letter, though modesty and shame forbade me to ask it of my maid, especially for the words that had passed between us. (*Elizabethan Love Stories*, p. 133)

50 *o'erlooked*: Perused.

52 *to a fault*: To commit a fault.

53 *What 'fool*: F's apostrophe would appear to indicate the omission of the indirect article.

55–6 *Since maids, in modesty, say no . . . the profferer construe*
     ay: An Elizabethan proverb.
56 *construe*: Accented on the first syllable.
58 *testy*: Fretful.
59 *presently*: Immediately.
62 *angerly*: Angrily.
68 *kill*: Allay, satisfy, subdue.
     stomach: The pun is on 'appetite' and 'anger'.
69 *maid*: There is probably a pun here with *meat*, which
     was often pronounced 'mate'.
70–100 *What is't that you took up so gingerly . . . papers lie*: This
     is very close to a passage in *La Diana* where Felismena
     (Julia) describes the episode with her maid:

> . . . the discreet and subtle Rosina came into my chamber to
> help me to make me ready; in doing whereof, of purpose she
> let the letter closely fall; which when I perceived: 'What is
> that that fell down?' said I. 'Let me see it.' 'It is nothing,
> mistress,' said she. 'Come, come, let me see it,' said I. 'What!
> move me not, or else tell me what it is.' 'Good Lord, mistress,'
> said she, 'why will you see it? It is the letter I would have
> given you yesterday.' 'Nay, that it is not,' said I, 'wherefore
> show it me, that I may see if you lie or no.' I had no sooner
> said so but she put it into my hands, saying: 'God never give
> me good if it be any other thing.' And although I knew it
> well indeed, yet I said: 'What, this is not the same; for I know
> that well enough. But it is one of thy lover's letters. I will
> read it, to see in what need he standeth of thy favour.'
> (*Elizabethan Love Stories*, p. 134)

77 *lie*: Deceive, making a quibble with *lie* meaning 'remain'
     at 76.
     concerns: Is of importance.
80–96 *That I might sing it, madam . . . unruly bass*: All the
     quibbles in this exchange are based on the musical termi-
     nology of the period. See the subsequent notes for the
     meanings of individual terms.
81 *note*: The quibble is on 'letter' and 'musical note'.
     set: 'Write' (a letter) and 'set to music'.

82 *As little by*: Julia picks up the word *set* at 81 and turns it to mean 'set as little (store) by'.
   toys: Trifles.

83 *'Light o'love'*: A popular tune of the period, to which Shakespeare also refers in *Much Ado About Nothing*, III.4.39.

84 *It is too heavy for so light a tune*: It is too important or weighty in content for a tune which is trivial in having no 'burden'.

85 *burden*: 'Load' and 'musical refrain or figure repeated throughout the song in the bass'. There is also a bawdy allusion to 'a woman's burden'.

87 *I cannot reach so high*: 'It is beyond the range of my singing voice' and 'Proteus is of too high a social rank for a servant like me'.

89 *tune*: 'Correct musical pitch' and 'mood, humour'.

91 *sharp*: In keeping with the wordplay, Lucetta refers here (1) to the musical notation and (2) to some piece of stage business performed by Julia, such as a slap or pinch, to make Lucetta release the letter.

93 *flat*: 'The musical notation' and 'downright in attitude'.

94 *descant*: The reference is both to musical variations and to the variations of mood passed through by Julia.

95 *wanteth*: Needs, lacks.
   mean: Tenor. Lucetta obviously means Proteus here, and there is possibly a pun with 'man'.

96 *bass*: 'Bass part of a song' and 'base' or 'low (conduct)'.

97 *bid the bass*: The phrase is from a game called 'Prisoner's Base' in which a member of one team challenges the members of an opposite team to pursue him, thus giving the prisoner at base a chance to escape. Lucetta sees herself and Julia as opposing team members with Proteus as the prisoner at base.

98 *babble*: There may be a pun here with the word 'bauble', meaning the letter.

99 *a coil with protestation*: A fuss over a declaration of love.

102–3 *She makes it strange . . . with another letter*: This is clearly intended by Lucetta as an address to the audi-

ence. However, Julia's line 104 indicates that she over-
hears her maid's remark, and so many editors do not
mark the speech as an aside.

102 *makes it strange*: Pretends a lack of interest, displays
indifference.

104 *Nay, would I were so angered with the same*: Some editors
have transferred this line to Lucetta by stressing the *I*.
However, it is clear that Julia is merely regretting that
she has torn the letter.

106 *Injurious*: Unjust.

wasps: Her fingers.

108 *several*: Separate.

110 *As*: Thus.

115 *throughly*: Thoroughly.

116 *search*: Probe, cleanse (and thus 'cure'). Julia uses a
medical term in keeping with the *wound* at 115.

121 *ragged*: Rugged.

fearful, hanging: Some editors make this phrase a
compound adjective. The reference is probably to the
Tarpeian Rock from which traitors were cast in ancient
Rome.

124 *forlorn*: The accent is on the first syllable.

126 *sith*: Since.

131 *stays*: Waits.

134 *respect*: Set value on, prize.

best to take: It were best you take.

135 *taken up*: Rebuked.

136 *for*: For fear of.

137 *a month's mind*: A strong inclination, a keen desire.
Originally this was a mass said in memory of someone
a month after his death, but later it came to refer to the
desire for various foodstuffs characteristic of women
in the last month of pregnancy. The word *month* has
two syllables here, and was often spelt 'moneth'.

139 *wink*: Close my eyes (to them).

I.3

0 *Panthino*: This is the commonest form of the name in
F, although it is spelled *Panthion* at some points.
However, the spelling *Panthino* in F at I.3.76 indicates

that the *Panthino* form is the correct one.

1 *sad*: Serious.

2 *cloister*: Not necessarily a cathedral or monastery cloister, as the word was used to describe a colonnaded structure attached to other buildings.

4–16 *He wondered that your lordship . . . in his youth*: This is an elaboration of the idea noted at I.1.2. The parallel passage in *La Diana* is:

> his father . . . sent him to the great Princess Augusta Caesarina's court, telling him it was not meet that a young gentleman, and of so noble a house as he was, should spend his youth idly at home, where nothing could be learned but examples of vice. (*Elizabethan Love Stories*, p. 136)

5 *suffer*: Allow.

6 *of slender reputation*: Inconsequential, unimportant.

7 *Put forth*: Send abroad.

12 *meet*: Fitted.

13 *importune*: Urge; accented on the second syllable.

15 *impeachment*: Discredit, reproach.

18 *hammering*: Pondering.

23 *perfected*: Accented on the first syllable.

24 *were I best*: Would it be best for me.

27 *Emperor*: Elsewhere in the text and in the list of characters in F he is called a duke. See An Account of the Text.

30 *tilts and tournaments*: A tilt was a mock battle between two knights and a tournament was one between two parties of knights. In *La Diana* Don Felix (Proteus) makes manifest his love for Felismena (Julia) 'by sundry signs, as by tilt and tourneys' (*Elizabethan Love Stories*, p. 132).

31 *discourse*: Accented on the second syllable.

32 *be in eye*: Have the opportunity of witnessing.

33 *Worthy*: Worthy of.

42 *commend*: Commit.

44 *in good time*: A phrase frequently used when a person arrives opportunely.

break with him: Broach the matter to him.

47 *pawn*: Pledge.

48 *applaud*: Approve of.

53 *commendations*: Greetings, remembrances.

58 *gracèd*: Honoured.

60 *stand you affected*: Are you disposèd.

63 *sorted with*: Corresponding to, in agreement with.

64 *Muse*: Wonder.

69 *exhibition*: Allowance of money for maintenance.

71 *Excuse it not*: Do not make excuses (to evade the decision).

peremptory: Determined; accented on the first syllable.

72 *provided*: Equipped.

74 *Look what*: Whatever.

75 *No more of stay*: No more talk of preventing (your departure).

81 *take exceptions*: Make objections.

83 *excepted . . . against*: Objected . . . to.

84 *resembleth*: Pronounced here with four syllables.

91 *it answers*: F's *it answer's* may indicate that the sense intended was 'its answer is'.

II.1

2 *but one*: The quibble is with *on* in line 1. The two words were often spelt the same and could presumably be pronounced similarly.

11 *still*: Always.

13 *Go to*: An expression of annoyance.

17–30 *Marry, by these special marks . . . my master*: Speed describes ironically most of the attitudes attributed to the lover. See I.1.29–35. Cf. *As You Like It*, III.2.358–66.

18 *wreathe*: Fold.

18–19 *like a malcontent*: Folded arms were a posture often associated with the melancholy man.

19 *relish*: Sing, warble.

like a robin-redbreast: There is no obvious reason why this bird should be singled out for association with a love-song. Perhaps the meaning intended is that Valentine spends his time alone and disconsolate like a robin in winter.

21 *A B C*: A primer or horn-book used for teaching children to read.

21–2 *to weep, like a young wench that had buried her grandam*: A common proverb of the time.

22 *grandam*: Grandmother.

23 *takes diet*: Is dieting for health purposes.
   watch: Lie awake.

24 *puling*: Whiningly.
   like a beggar at Hallowmas: All Saints' Day or All-Hallows (1 November) was traditionally a feast on which paupers received special alms.

26 *like one of the lions*: This has been taken variously as an allusion to the lions kept at the Tower of London or to the heraldic lions on the royal standard which may have been displayed in theatres.

27 *presently*: Immediately.

28 *want*: Lack.
   metamorphosed: Changed in shape. Proteus applies the same word to himself at I.1.66.

29 *with*: By.
   that: So that.

32 *without*: Outside.

33 *Without me*: In my absence.

34 *without*: Unless.

35 *would*: Would perceive them. Dr Johnson suggested the meaning 'would be so simple'.
   without: The two meanings implied are 'lacking' and 'outside'.

37 *urinal*: A transparent glass container used by doctors in testing a patient's urine.

46 *hard-favoured*: Ugly.

47 *Not so fair, boy, as well-favoured*: Silvia's beauty is surpassed by her charm of manner.

50 *well favoured*: Looked on with favour.

52 *favour*: Charm, graciousness.

53 *painted*: The reference is to cosmetics.

54 *out of all count*: Beyond calculation, boundless.

57 *counts of*: Takes account of, esteems.

58 *account of*: Appreciate.

60 *deformed*: Speed's point is that the lover sees the appearance of the beloved falsely. Valentine takes the word to mean 'misshapen'.

67 *Love is blind*: The allusion is to blind Cupid and to the power of self-deception in the lover.

68 *lights*: Powers to see clearly.

69 *going ungartered*: This was considered one of the signs of the lovesick man; cf. *As You Like It*, III.2.363.

73 *to put on your hose*: Speed is indicating that Valentine is in a worse state than Proteus, for whereas Proteus had difficulty only with the gartering of his hose, Valentine has difficulty with the hose themselves. There have been many emendations proposed for this phrase (see the second list of collations), all of which change the point being made.

77 *swinged*: Thrashed.

79 *stand affected to*: Am in love with. See note to 80.

80 *set*: Seated. Speed takes up the normal meaning of Valentine's *stand* at 79. There is also a bawdy jest intended by Speed in that he takes *stand* also to mean 'a sexual erection' and suggests by *set* 'put down' which would thus make his master less love-sick.

86 *lamely*: Not scanned correctly, lacking the correct number of metrical feet.

89 *motion*: A puppet show, or, sometimes, a single puppet.

90 *Now will he interpret to her*: The puppeteer not only manipulated the dolls in the play but also provided a commentary which 'interpreted' the action.

93 *give ye*: God give you.

95 *servant*: A term of the courtly love convention, applied to any man paying attentions to a lady who had not committed herself to choosing him as her lover.

102 *clerkly*: In a scholarly fashion, or, perhaps, with good penmanship.

103 *came hardly off*: Was difficult to perform.

107 *stead*: Benefit, assist.

110 *period*: Full pause.

112 *again*: Back.

116 *quaintly*: Skilfully, with ingenuity.

134 *reasoning*: Discussing, talking of.

140 *by a figure*: Indirectly. The term is from rhetoric.

147–8 *perceive her earnest*: The quibble is on 'see that she was serious' and 'see the sum she paid to bind a bargain'.

152–3 *there an end*: There is nothing more to say about the matter.

160 *speak in print*: Speak precisely or exactly.

in print I found it: The phrase is difficult to explain. The second *in print* should be some kind of pun on the first *in print* ('plainly'). Speed seems to be claiming that his doggerel fourteeners are a quotation from some book or ballad, so possibly they should be printed as a quotation and many editors do this. However, they have not been traced.

161 *muse*: Ponder.

162 *I have dined*: Valentine implies he has feasted on the sight of Silvia.

163–4 *the chameleon Love can feed on the air*: The belief that the chameleon existed like this was a common one. Love was often called a chameleon because of the changeability of lovers.

166 *be moved*: The quibble is on 'have compassion' and 'be persuaded to go (to dinner)'.

II.2

If Shakespeare did use *La Diana* as his source, then this scene marks a departure from the story where Felix (Proteus) 'went away so pensive that his great grief would not suffer him' to inform Felismena (Julia) of his departure (*Elizabethan Love Stories*, p. 136).

2 *where is*: Where there is.

4 *turn not*: Are not inconstant, do not prove unfaithful.

6–8 *Why, then, we'll make exchange . . . true constancy*: Although there is no witness present Proteus and Julia are going through the forms of the betrothal ceremony: the joining of hands and the sealing kiss.

9 *o'erslips*: Passes by unnoticed.

14 *The tide is now*: The tide is right for sailing. See note to I.1.54.

tide of tears: Flood of tears. Cf. the parody of these

words at II.3.31–51.

17 *Ay, so true love should do; it cannot speak*: This is ironical in view of Proteus's loquaciousness and subsequent unfaithfulness.

19 *I come*: F reads *I come, I come*. However, as it is obvious
that a rhymed couplet is intended to end the scene, I
have assumed the F reading to be due to a simple error
of repetition on the part of the compositor.

II.3

0 *with his dog, Crab*: Dogs were not frequently used as
actors on the Elizabethan stage, although there are other
examples of scenes requiring them.

1–30 *Nay, 'twill be this hour . . . with my tears*: For the dramatic
relevance of this monologue to II.2 and to the love plot
in general, see Introduction, pp. xl–xli.

2 *kind*: Family, kindred.
this very: Exactly this.

3 *proportion*: A malapropism for 'portion'.
prodigious: A malapropism for 'prodigal'.

4 *Imperial's*: Emperor's. See note to I.3.27.

5 *sourest-natured*: The reference is to the dog's name
Crab, meaning 'crab-apple'.

13 *parting*: Departure.

16 *the worser sole*: The reference is to the common medieval
debate as to whether a woman's soul was inferior to a
man's.
sole: The quibble is on 'sole of the shoe' and 'soul'.

17 *This shoe with the hole in it*: Thus, the *worser sole* and
also a bawdy reference to the female sex organ.

20 *small*: Slim.

26 *an old woman*: F has *a would-woman*. The commonest
emendation is 'a wood woman' (meaning 'a mad
woman'), but this is inappropriate in the context and
it is difficult to see how such an error came about.
Another suggestion is 'a wold woman' (meaning 'a
country woman'). However, if Shakespeare had written
'a nould woman' the F reading would be understandable as a misprint for 'a nould' meaning 'an old'. The
comic business is fairly clear: Launce makes the shoe

representing his mother give out a squeaking sound *up and down* like an asthmatic old woman. He admits that the imitation is not a perfect one, and by manipulating the shoe makes it more plausible.

27–8 *up and down*: Exactly. It has also been suggested that the reference is to the lacing of the shoe.

28–9 *Mark the moan she makes*: Launce presumably swishes the staff through the air as he says this.

30 *lay the dust*: Keep down the dust (by sprinkling it with tears).

32 *post*: Hasten.

35, 36 *tied*: The dog which is *tied*. The F spelling is *tide*.

44 *lose*: The two meanings suggested are 'lose' and 'loose, release'.

45–6 *Where should I lose my tongue . . . In thy tale*: A common bawdy gibe which Shakespeare also uses in *The Taming of the Shrew*, II.1.213–15.

49 *and the tied*: Launce may here 'loose' the dog; *loose* is the spelling form of both 'lose' and 'loose' in F.

52 *call*: Summon.

54 *call me*: In his usual way Launce mistakes Panthino's *call* to mean 'call names'.

II.4

1 *Servant*: See note to II.1.95.

7 *knocked*: Struck.
Exit: This does not occur in F, but it is clearly impracticable in terms of staging to have the clown on the stage during the subsequent exchange between the other characters, although some editors allow him to remain. See An Account of the Text.

12 *counterfeits*: Cheats.

18 *quote*: Observe, note. The word was often written and pronounced 'cote', which enables Valentine to pun with 'coat' (*jerkin*) at 19.

20 *jerkin . . . doublet*: Articles of Elizabethan clothing; the jerkin was a long jacket worn over a doublet or in place of it, the doublet was a short and loose coat-like garment.

21 *double*: The pun is with *doublet* (double it).

22 *How*: An expression of surprise or annoyance.

27 *live in your air*: See note to II.1.163–4.

34 *giver*: Direction-giver (technically a person who directed an archer's or gunner's aim).

36 *fire*: Valentine maintains the shooting allusions suggested by Silvia's *volley of words* at 32.

38 *kindly*: Of natural affection or gratitude.

43 *liveries*: Uniforms worn by a gentleman's servants.

51 *happy messenger*: Bringer of good news.

54 *worthy*: Worthy of.

55 *without desert*: Undeservingly.

61 *conversed*: Associated.

63 *Omitting*: Neglecting, letting slip.

68 *unmellowed*: Not tinged with grey hair.

70 *Comes*: The singular verb form with a plural subject is frequent in Shakespeare's grammar.

71 *feature*: Person, physical appearance.

73 *Beshrew me*: A mild oath used for emphasis.

75 *meet*: Fitted.

83 *cite*: Urge, summon. This F reading is sometimes taken to be an abbreviation of 'incite' or 'excite' both of which are incorrect.

84 *presently*: Now.

88 *Belike*: It is likely.
   enfranchised: Set free.

89 *pawn for fealty*: Pledge for fidelity.

94 *Love hath not an eye at all*: See note to II.1.67.

96 *homely*: Plain.
   wink: Shut the eye.

102 *entertain*: Take into service.

107 *discourse*: Accented on the second syllable.

110 *want*: Lack.
    meed: Reward.

112 *die on him*: Challenge him to mortal combat, die fighting him.

113 *Enter a Servant*: In F line 114 is given to Thurio. Such a reading requires that he exit some time earlier and re-enter here, which is how many editors solve the difficulty. Silvia's line 115 appears to be addressed to

two separate people and so I have introduced the servant
to issue the summons to Silvia from her father. The
silence of Thurio in the preceding lines is certainly an
unsatisfactory aspect of the scene but not altogether
surprising in view of the fool he is.

121 *have them much commended*: Have sent their kind
remembrances.

127 *contemning*: Despising.

128 *high imperious thoughts*: Cupid's imperiousness in
dealing with lovers was sufficiently commonplace to
make the F reading acceptable, although it has been
suggested that the phrase is not appropriate and that the
manuscript from which F was set may have had
'thonges'.

135 *as*: That.

136 *to*: Comparable to.

142 *Was this the idol that you worship so*: This is ironical in
view of Proteus's desire in IV.2.116–22 to worship
Silvia's portrait.

149 *by her*: Of her.

150 *principality*: This refers to the seventh order in the
Christian hierarchy of divine beings below God. Dr
Johnson with great ingenuity took the phrase to mean
'the first and principal of women'.

152 *Sweet*: This was a general term of affection applicable
to men as well as women.

153 *Except*: Unless.
    except against: Take exception to, object to.

155 *prefer*: Promote, advance in station. Valentine is quibbling on Proteus's *prefer* (meaning 'have a preference
for') at 154.

160 *to root*: To receive the roots of.

163 *can*: Can say.

165 *alone*: Peerless, unique.

170 *dream on thee*: Think about your feelings.

173 *for*: Because.

184 *inquire you forth*: Seek you out, ask after your where-
abouts.

185 *road*: See note to I.1.53.

187 *presently*: Immediately.

190–93 *Even as one heat another heat expels . . . quite forgotten*:
Arthur Brooke's poem *The Tragical History of Romeus
and Juliet* (1562), which has been suggested as a possible
source for part of the play, has: 'And as out of a plank
a nail a nail doth drive, | So novel love out of the mind
the ancient love doth rive.'

194 *Is it mine eye, or Valentine's praise*: F's *It is mine,
or Valentine's praise* needs some emendation, the error
having come about possibly through some cutting of
the text, for the details of which see An Account of
the Text. For other suggested emendations, see the
second list of collations. See also headnote to II.6.

205, 206 *advice*: Knowledge.

207 *'Tis but her picture I have yet beheld*: If *picture* means
'portrait' here, then clearly there is something wrong
with the text. Some editors explain away the difficulty
by taking the word to mean 'outward appearance' as
opposed to 'mind' (inner qualities). However, this is
unacceptable in view of 209. For a possible explanation of the origin of the difficulty, see An Account of
the Text.

208 *dazzlèd*: Pronounced with three syllables.

210 *no reason but*: No doubt that.

212 *compass*: Obtain, win.

II.5

1 *Milan*: F has *Padua* which is clearly erroneous. For
details of the confused geography of the play, see An
Account of the Text.

3 *undone*: Ruined.

5 *shot*: Tavern-reckoning, account.
hostess: Hostess of a tavern.

8 *presently*: At once.

10 *part with*: Take leave of.

11 *closed*: The quibble is on 'came to terms' and
'embraced'.

17 *are they broken*: Have they fallen out? is their affair
broken off?

18 *as whole as a fish*: Quite sound.

19 *how stands the matter with them*: What is the state of affairs between them?

20–21 *when it stands well with him, it stands well with her*: Launce answers Speed's question literally: 'what is agreeable to him is likewise agreeable to her', but he also makes a bawdy joke by means of a quibble: 'when he has a sexual erection she is pleased by it'.

23 *block*: Blockhead.

23–4 *My staff understands me*: With some bawdy gesture Launce illustrates his quibble at 20–21.

26 *lean*: The quibble is on 'to put one's weight on' and 'to incline in thought, affection or conduct'.

27 *understands*: The quibble is on 'supports' and 'comprehends'.

35 *by a parable*: Indirectly.

36–7 *how sayest thou that my master is become*: What have you got to say about the fact that my master has become.

40 *lubber*: A large stupid man, with a pun on *lover*.

41 *whoreson*: A coarse pleasantry.
   thou mistakest me: You misunderstand me.

42–3 *I meant not thee, I meant thy master*: Launce thinks Speed is using *mistakest* with the meaning 'mistake Speed for Valentine'.

46 *If thou wilt, go with me to the alehouse*: The insertion of the comma after *wilt* makes good sense of the F line. There is no need, as some editors have done, to emend by following F2 and using *If thou wilt go with me to the alehouse, so.*

51 *the ale*: A 'Church-ale' or a 'Holy-ale', which were parish festivals (and thus *Christian*) at which ale was made and sold to raise church funds.

II.6

It has been suggested that Shakespeare in this scene was influenced by a passage in Sir Thomas Elyot's *The Book of the Governor* where the story of Titus and Gisippus is told. Titus falls in love with Gisippus's mistress, Sophronia:

But Titus forthwith as he beheld so heavenly a personage

adorned with beauty inexplicable, in whose visage was most amiable countenance mixed with maidenly shame-facedness . . . was thereat abashed, and had the heart through pierced with the fiery dart of blind Cupid. Of the which wound the anguish was so exceeding and vehement, that neither the study of philosophy, neither the remembrance of his dear friend Gisippus, who so much loved and trusted him, could anything withdraw him from that unkind appetite, but that of force he must love inordinately that lady, whom his said friend had determined to marry. Albeit with incredible pains he kept his thoughts secret. (p. 213)

1, 2 *forsworn*: Followed in this edition by semicolons, although F and some modern editors punctuate with question marks. However, Proteus is rather pondering what he intends to do and the implications of his actions than asking himself whether he should do so or not.

7 *sweet-suggesting*: Sweetly tempting, seductive.

12 *wit*: Sense.

13 *learn*: Teach.

17 *leave to love*: Stop loving.

26 *Ethiope*: A common Elizabethan word for a black African, and was often used by Shakespeare as the antithesis of the English ideal of fair-skinned beauty. Cf. *A Midsummer Night's Dream*, III.2.257; *Much Ado About Nothing*, V.4.38.

35 *competitor*: Associate, confederate.

37 *pretended*: Intended.

40 *cross*: Thwart.

41 *blunt*: Stupid.
   dull: Obtuse.

43 *wit*: Ingenuity.
   drift: Scheme.

II.7

The parallel passage in *La Diana* is where Felismena (Julia) says she

determined to adventure that which I think never any woman imagined: which was to apparel myself in the habit of a man,

and to hie me to the court to see him in whose sight all my
hope and content remained. Which determination I no sooner
thought of than I put in practice, love blinding my eyes and
mind with an inconsiderate regard of mine own estate and
condition. To the execution of which attempt I wanted no
industry. For, being furnished with the help of one of my
approved friends and treasuress of my secrets, who bought
me such apparel as I willed her and a good horse for my
journey, I went not only out of my country but out of my
dear reputation; which I think I shall never recover again.
And so trotted directly to the court, passing by way many
accidents. (*Elizabethan Love Stories*, pp. 136–7).

Cf. the similar scene between Portia and Nerissa in *The
Merchant of Venice* (III.4).

2 *conjure*: Beseech, adjure; accented on the first syllable.

3 *table*: Tablet for memoranda.

4 *charactered*: Inscribed, written; accented on the second
syllable.

5 *lesson*: Teach.
mean: Method.

6 *with my honour*: While preserving my honour.

9 *true-devoted pilgrim*: This is another example of the religious love-vocabulary of the play. Cf. Valentine's
words at I.1.52 and II.4.143–51.

9–10 *weary | To measure*: Weary in traversing.

16 *dearth*: Scarcity, famine.

18 *inly*: Inward.

22 *fire's*: Two syllables.

24 *The more thou dammest it up, the more it burns*: Some
editors have taken exception to the mixed metaphor
here, although *dammest* could quite easily mean the
'banking' or 'piling up' of a fire with fuel.

28 *enamelled*: Variegated.

29 *sedge*: Plant.

32 *wild*: Some editors have found the word (in its meaning
'tempestuous') inappropriate because Julia parallels the
ocean with her love, where like the *stream* she will *rest
as . . . A blessèd soul doth in Elysium*. However, the

word also meant simply 'open, wide, unenclosed'.

ocean: Pronounced with three syllables here.

38 *Elysium*: In Greek mythology, the abode of the blessed after death.

39 *habit*: Dress, clothing.

40 *prevent*: Avoid (by taking preventative action).

41 *encounters*: Accostings.

42 *weeds*: Garments.

43 *beseem*: Be suitable for, be appropriate to.

46 *odd-conceited*: Elaborately odd.

47 *fantastic*: Fanciful, capricious.

48 *greater time*: Older years.

show: Appear.

51 *compass*: Circumference.

farthingale: Hooped petticoat.

53 *must needs*: Will have to.

codpiece: A bagged covering over the male genitals at the front of close-fitting breeches.

54 *ill-favoured*: Ill-looking, unbecoming.

55 *round hose*: Breeches which covered both the loins and legs and puffed out at the hips.

not worth a pin: Not at all valued.

56 *to stick pins on*: One of the uses to which the codpiece was put.

58 *meet*: Suitable, appropriate.

59 *how will the world repute me*: What will people think of my action.

60 *unstaid*: Immodest.

61 *scandalized*: Disgraced, subject to scandal.

64 *infamy*: Discredit.

66 *No matter*: It does not matter.

67 *withal*: With it.

70 *of infinite of love*: There is no need for emendation here, as *infinite* as a noun meaning 'infinity' was common at the time.

74–81 *But truer stars did govern Proteus' birth . . . his truth*: Note how the dramatic effectiveness of this is heightened by its following immediately on Proteus's soliloquy in II.6.

74 *truer stars did govern Proteus' birth*: The allusion is to
the belief that a man's character was determined by the
astrological signs under which he was born.

79 *prove so*: Turn out to be so.

81 *hard*: Bad.

83 *presently*: Immediately.

85 *longing*: Prompted by longing.

86 *at thy dispose*: In your charge, at your disposal.

87 *reputation*: Pronounced with five syllables.

90 *tarriance*: Delay.

III.1

1 *give us leave*: A courteous form of dismissal.

2 *Exit Thurio*: This stage direction appears necessary
although it does not appear in F. The entry and imme-
diate exit of Thurio here appear purposeless, and have
been adduced as evidence for the F text being a cut
version of the play; see An Account of the Text.

4 *discover*: Disclose, reveal.

8 *pricks me on*: Urges me.

12 *am one made privy to*: Am one of the secret participants
in.

18 *drift*: Scheme, purpose.

21 *timeless*: Untimely.

25 *Haply*: By chance.

28 *jealous aim*: Suspicious guess.

34 *suggested*: Tempted, led astray.

35 *upper tower*: The upper storey of a tower.

36 *ever*: Always.

38 *mean*: Method.

40 *corded ladder*: Rope-ladder.

42 *presently*: Immediately.

45 *discovery*: Disclosure.
aimèd at: Guessed.

46 *For*: For, is the punctuation of F, indicating that the
word means 'because' here. The large majority of
modern editors omit the comma.

47 *publisher*: One who exposes or brings to light.
pretence: Scheme, intention.

49 *light*: Information.

55 *of much import*: Of great significance; the accent in
   import is on the second syllable.

57 *happy being*: Agreeable life.

59 *break with thee of*: Disclose to you.

60 *touch me near*: Are of importance to me.

66 *Beseeming*: Befitting.

67 *fancy*: Love.

68 *peevish*: Foolishly wayward.
   froward: Refractory, rebellious, perverse.

70 *regarding*: Taking due notice.

73 *Upon advice*: On reflection, on consideration.

74 *where*: Whereas.

77 *who*: Whoever.

81 *of Verona*: F has *in Verona*, which is obviously incorrect. Many editors have attempted to solve the difficulty
   by substituting some form of 'Milan' that will not affect
   the metre (see the second list of collations). I find this
   reading preferable as it gives the Duke a motive for
   approaching Valentine, another Veronese, on the
   subject.

82 *affect*: Am fond of.
   nice: Fastidious.

84 *to*: As, for.

85 *agone*: Ago.
   forgot: Forgotten how.

87 *bestow*: Conduct, deport.

89 *respect not*: Takes no heed of.

90–105 *Dumb jewels . . . win a woman*: Note the change to
   rhymed couplets as the subject matter of the dialogue
   moves to the topic of Petrarchistic love-making. This
   is a more simple use of the device employed in *Romeo
   and Juliet* (I.5.93–106) where the lovers' initial exchange
   takes the form of a sonnet.

90 *kind*: Nature.

91 *quick*: Lively or living (as opposed to the *Dumb* jewels
   of 90).

93 *contents*: Pleases, delights.

99 *For why*: Because.

99–101 *the fools are mad if left alone . . . doth not mean 'Away!'*:

This appears to have been influenced by John Lyly's play *Sapho and Phao*:

We are mad wenches, if men mark our words; for when I say, I would none cared for love more than I, what mean I but I would none loved but I? Where we cry 'away', do we not presently say 'go to'; and when men strive for kisses, we exclaim, 'let us alone', as though we would fall to that ourselves. (I.4.43–7)

99 *fools*: A term of affection at the time.

101 *For*: By.

102–5 *Flatter and praise, commend, extol their graces . . . a woman*: John Lyly elaborates the idea in a similar way in *Sapho and Phao*:

Flatter I mean lie . . . Imagine with thyself all are to be won . . . It is unpossible for the brittle metal of women to withstand the flattering attempts of men . . . Be prodigal in praises . . . There is none so foul, that thinketh not herself fair. In commending thou canst lose no labour; for of every one thou shalt be believed. (II.4.60–71)

103 *black*: Dark-complexioned, and thus, by contemporary English standards of beauty, not fair-skinned, not beautiful.

104, 105 *no man . . . woman*: A rhyme is almost certainly intended here.

109 *That*: So that.

110 *I would*: I advise, I recommend.

112 *That*: So that.

113 *lets*: Hinders, prevents.

115 *shelving*: Overhanging.

116 *apparent*: Obvious, evident, manifest.

117 *quaintly*: Deftly, skilfully.

119–20 *another Hero's tower . . . Leander would adventure it*: See note to I.1.22.

120 *So*: Provided.
     adventure: Venture

121 *of blood*: Of good parentage. The phrase could also mean 'spirited', which is appropriate here.

130 *of any length*: Tolerably long.

131 *turn*: Occasion.

133 *such another*: A similar.

138 *engine*: Contrivance, instrument (the rope-ladder).
proceeding: Scheme.

140–49 *My thoughts do harbour with my Silvia nightly . . . should be*: The form of this poem suggests a regular Shakespearian sonnet without the final quatrain.

140–41 *My thoughts do harbour with my Silvia nightly,* | *And slaves they are to me, that send them flying*: Cf. Sonnet 27: 'For then my thoughts, from far where I abide, | Intend a zealous pilgrimage to thee.'

140 *harbour*: Lodge.

142 *lightly*: Easily.

143 *senseless*: Insensible (of the honour).

144 *herald*: Bearing messages.
in thy pure bosom: The reference here is to the small pocket which Elizabethan women's gowns had located in the inside of the bodice between the breasts. It is frequently alluded to as a receptacle for letters, love-tokens and sentimental mementoes.

145 *importune*: Command; accented on the second syllable.

146 *grace . . . grace*: Graciousness . . . favour. There may be in the first *grace* a quibble with 'one of the Graces'.

147 *want*: Lack.

148 *I curse myself, for they are sent by me*: In cursing them I am cursing myself who sent them (to the coveted resting-place).

153–5 *Why, Phaethon . . . Merops' son . . . the world*: Phaethon was the son of Phoebus, the sun god, by Clymene, the wife of Merops. He persuaded his father to let him drive the sun chariot, and, being unable to control the horses, allowed the chariot to come too near the earth. It has been suggested that there is a pun intended on *Merops* and 'ropes'.

156 *Wilt thou reach stars, because they shine on thee*: A common proverb.

157 *overweening*: Presumptuous.

158 *mates*: Used scornfully here.

160 *Is privilege for*: Grants the privilege of.

164 *expedition*: Haste, dispatch.

170–87 *And why not death, rather than living torment . . . from life*: This is very similar in wording and sentiment to Romeo's complaint to Friar Laurence when he is banished for killing Tybalt in *Romeo and Juliet*, III.3.12–71: 'Ha, banishment? Be merciful, say "death". | For exile hath more terror in his look, | Much more than death' (12–14); 'There is no world without Verona walls, | . . . Hence banishèd is banished from the world, | . . . Heaven is here, | Where Juliet lives' (17, 19, 29–30).

175–7 *What joy is joy, if Silvia be not by . . . shadow of perfection*: This is exactly what Proteus elects to do in IV.2.116–22.

177 *shadow*: Illusion, image, idea.

182 *essence*: Very life.
     leave: Cease.

183 *influence*: The allusion is to the *influence* exerted by a star on human beings, which was the basis of astrological belief.

185–7 *I fly not death, to fly his deadly doom . . . from life*: Cf the similar quibbling in *Romeo and Juliet* (III.3.40–42, 44): 'This may flies do, when I from this must fly. | And sayest thou yet that exile is not death? | But Romeo may not, he is banishèd. . . . | They are free men. But I am banishèd.'

185 *I fly not death, to fly his deadly doom*: The meaning here is not altogether clear. Valentine may mean 'I do not escape death by running away from the Duke's sentence of death' or 'I do not escape death by flying away from death's deadly doom'.
     to fly: In flying.

186 *attend on*: Wait for.

187 At this point it has been suggested by some critics that an interval scene originally followed Valentine's soliloquy, because during these eighteen lines it is too much to believe that the Duke has issued a proclamation

(216–18), has interviewed Silvia (221–32) and has imprisoned his daughter in the tower (233–6).

189 *So-ho*: This was the hunter's cry when a hare was started.

191–2 *there's not a hair on's head but 'tis a Valentine*: Every hair on his head declares him for what he is: namely, a true lover.

191 *a hair*: Launce is punning on 'hare', which, with his cry at 189, he pretended to be hunting.

192 *a Valentine*: Launce quibbles on Valentine's name and its meaning, 'a token of true love'. Cf. 210–14.

208 *they*: News is being thought of as plural.

211 *No Valentine*: The quibble is on 'no longer myself' and 'no true love'.

216 *proclamation*: The proclamation of Valentine's banishment, Silvia's interview with her father and her imprisonment in the tower have all taken place in the time covered by Valentine's soliloquy at 170–87. This has persuaded some editors that the text has been cut at this point; see An Account of the Text. However, it should be noticed that there are similar time anomalies in Shakespeare's other plays.

vanished: A malapropism for 'banished'.

220 *surfeit*: Sicken from overabundance.

222 *doom*: Sentence.

233 *chafed*: Irritated, enraged.

234 *repeal*: Recall.

240 *anthem*: Song of grief, requiem.

247 *manage*: Handle, wield.

250 *Even in the milk-white bosom*: See note to 144.

251 *expostulate*: Discuss, expatiate.

255 *though not for thyself*: Even though not for your own sake.

256 *Regard*: Take notice of.

262–3 *but that's all one if he be but one knave*: Behind Launce's remark seems to lie the proverb 'Two knaves need no broker'. 'Two knaves' was a common term in reference to excessive knavery at the time (cf. *Othello*, I.3.388: 'double knavery'). Some editors have thought

the reference may be to Proteus – a knave to both his
mistress and his friend.

263–4 *He lives not now that knows me to be in love*: This may
be an allusion to Valentine's disclosure of his affairs to
Proteus.

264 *horse*: Horses.

267–8 *yet 'tis not a maid, for she hath had gossips*: *Gossips* were
originally a child's baptismal sponsors; however, the
word came to mean in common parlance 'women
friends invited to attend a birth'. Launce implies that
his inamorata is not a virgin (*maid*) as she has had an
illegitimate child.

268 *maid*: Servant, the quibble being with *maid* (meaning
'virgin') at 267.

269–70 *more qualities than a water-spaniel*: The spaniel was
proverbial for its fawning. The many uses of the water-
spaniel are listed in Dr Caius's *Treatise on English Dogs*
(1576), among which are the capacity to find hidden
duck by the smell, to locate and recover spent bolts and
arrows which have dropped into the water, and to bring
back to the hunter both the ducks he has shot and the
ducks killed by other means.

270 *bare*: Launce implies the two meanings: 'mere' and
'naked' (as opposed to the hair-covered spaniel).

271 *cate-log*: Catalogue. Some editors modernize the
spelling, pointing out correctly that 'catlog' was a recognized spelling at the time. However, there are the possi-
bilities that (1) the spelling was intended to indicate
Launce's pronunciation, and (2) a quibble is intended
with 'cates' (meaning 'dainties').
condition: Qualities.

271–4 *Imprimis . . . carry . . . Item . . . milk*: The form adopted
here is that of the usual Elizabethan inventory of goods.

272–3 *a horse cannot fetch*: The verb means 'go and bring'
which a horse cannot be ordered to do.

274 *jade*: Launce quibbles on 'a woman of low morals' and
'a mare in bad physical condition'.

278 *master's ship*: F has *Mastership*, but the pun is obviously
intended.

at sea: The quibble is on 'afloat' and 'awry'.

279 *old vice still*: It has been suggested that there is an allusion here to the Vice (a combination of clown and
villain) of the old morality plays which were performed
in England up to the 1570s.

282 *black*: Bad.

284 *them*: See note to 208.

285 *jolt-head*: Blockhead, numbskull.

289 *loiterer*: Idler.

292 *Saint Nicholas be thy speed*: May St Nicholas help you!
(with a pun on Speed's name). St Nicholas was the
legendary patron saint of scholars.

293–4 *Imprimis: She can milk . . . Ay, that she can*: Launce is
quibbling on the second meaning of *milk*: 'to entice a
lover by wiles'. It is noticeable that Speed quotes differ-
ently from Launce so far as the beginning of the catalogue is concerned.

294 *can*: Possibly a pun on 'milk-can'.

301 *stock*: Dowry.

302 *knit him a stock*: Knit him a stocking or netherstock.
Launce is also playing on *knit* meaning 'conceive' and
stock which could mean both 'a stupid person' and 'a
line of descendants'.

305 *washed and scoured*: The quibble is on 'knocked down'
and 'beaten'.

307–8 *she can spin for her living*: The verb may carry a sexual
connotation as it does in *Twelfth Night*, I.3.99.

307 *set the world on wheels*: Live at ease, let things slide, be
independent.

309 *nameless*: Inexpressible, but carrying overtones also of
'too small to be worth detailed description'.

310 *bastard virtues*: Virtuous qualities of little value, inferior or base virtues.

313–14 *Here follow her vices . . . Close at the heels of her virtues*:
It is possible that this is an allusion to the alternating
Vice and Virtue scenes in the old morality plays.

313 *Here follow her vices*: Some editors take this to be a
quotation from Launce's catalogue.

315 *to be kissed fasting*: F reads *to be fasting*. It has been

suggested that the blank was left deliberately for the
clown to supply an ad lib indecency; but Launce's reply
seems to require this universally accepted emendation
from Rowe's edition of 1709.

in respect of: Owing to, on account of.

319 *a sweet mouth*: A wanton or lecherous nature. It is not
altogether clear whether Launce takes this literally to
mean 'a kissable mouth' which compensates for her bad
breath.

322–3 *sleep not in her talk*: Is not slow or stupid in her speech.
There is also a quibble intended on *sleep* and 'slip'
similar to that on *sheep* and 'ship' at I.1.73.

329 *it was Eve's legacy*: Launce may merely mean that pride
was the original deadly sin, or he may be taking *proud*
to mean 'hot-blooded, lascivious'.

332 *because I love crusts*: And will not have to share them
with her.

333 *curst*: Shrewish.

335 *praise*: Appraise, test (by sipping).

336 *If her liquor be good, she shall*: Launce takes *praise* to
mean 'laud'.

338 *liberal*: Bold, wanton, loose in her talk.

341 *another thing*: A sexual allusion.

343–4 *She hath more hair than wit, and more faults than hairs*:
It has been suggested that this is a parody of a passage
in John Lyly's *Euphues. The Anatomy of Wit* (1578):
'This young gallant of more wit than wealth, and yet
of more wealth than wisdom' (p. 1).

343 *more hair than wit*: A proverbial expression.

346 *Rehearse*: Repeat.

349–50 *the cover of the salt hides the salt*: The lid of the salt-
cellar conceals the salt. The quibble is on *salt* meaning
'wit'.

356 *gracious*: Acceptable.

360 *stays*: Waits.

366 *Thou must run to him*: Launce takes Speed's word *go* to
mean 'walk', which was a common Elizabethan
meaning.

stayed: Tarried.

367 *going*: Walking.

    serve the turn: Be appropriate.

370 *swinged*: Thrashed, beaten.

372 *correction*: Punishment.

III.2

3–5 *Since his exile . . . obtaining her*: It might be assumed from this that there has been a lapse of some time between III.1 and III.2; but it is clear from 11–13 that the time-lapse is but a few hours. The accent is on the second syllable in *exile*.

  5 *That*: So that.

    desperate: Without hope.

  6 *impress*: Accented on the second syllable.

  7 *Trenchèd*: Cut.

    hour's: Pronounced with two syllables here.

  8 *his*: Its.

    form: Shape.

14 *grievously*: Sorrowfully. Some copies of F have *heavily*, which is on the uncorrected version of the page.

17 *conceit*: Conception, opinion.

19 *better*: More ready, more willing.

28 *persevers*: Perseveres; accented on the second syllable.

35 *deliver*: Report.

36 *circumstance*: Much incidental detail, circumlocution.

41 *very friend*: True or special friend.

44 *is indifferent*: Counts neither way, is neither good nor bad.

45 *your friend*: The Duke.

49 *weed*: Weed out, root out. Chiefly because of Thurio's word *unwind* at 51, many editors have felt disposed to emend this word. The suggestions made include 'wind', 'wend' and 'woo'.

52 *ravel*: Become entangled.

53 *bottom it*: Wind it. A skein or ball of wool was wound on a core or 'bottom' of some harder material.

56 *in this kind*: In an affair of this kind.

58 *You are already Love's firm votary*: Note the irony.

60 *Upon this warrant*: In accordance with this command.

62 *lumpish*: Low-spirited, in the dumps.

64 *temper*: Mould, dispose.

67 *sharp*: Keen.

68 *lime*: Bird-lime. It is noticeable that Proteus's metaphor is one of trapping.

tangle: Ensnare.

70 *serviceable vows*: Devoted vows or vows of service.

77 *discover such integrity*: Disclose such true devotion. Some editors have hazarded that a line has been lost following this. However, *such* may refer to the devotion which would result if the advice in the foregoing lines was followed, or possibly to the tears used to moisten the ink.

78–81 *For Orpheus' lute was strung with poets' sinews . . . on sands*: The allusion is to the mythical Greek musician to whom were attributed the powers described.

78 *sinews*: Nerves.

81 *unsounded*: Unfathomable.

82 *elegies*: Love-poems.

83 *Visit*: Go with some accompaniment.

84 *consort*: Company of musicians (usually referring to those who performed part-songs); accented on the first syllable.

85 *dump*: Sad tune.

86 *grievance*: Grieving, grief or sorrowful affections.

87 *inherit*: Secure, gain possession of.

88 *This discipline shows thou hast been in love*: Note the irony in the use of the past tense of the verb.

discipline: Instruction, lesson.

90 *direction-giver*: See note to II.4.34.

91 *presently*: Immediately.

92 *sort*: Sort out, select.

94 *To give the onset to*: To make a beginning in following.

98 *Even now about it*: Do it immediately! (not after supper).

pardon you: Excuse your attendance on me.

IV.1

This scene obviously takes place in a forest on the outskirts of Milan and, presumably, in the direction of Verona.

1 *passenger*: Traveller.

4 *sit*: In weak antithesis to *stand* at 3.

  rifle: Plunder, search and rob.

5 *undone*: Come to grief.

10 *by my beard*: A common oath of the time.

  proper: Handsome, comely.

12 *crossed with*: Thwarted by.

20 *sixteen months*: An example of the confused time-scheme of the play, as it would entail a time-lapse of some fifteen months between I.1 and I.3.

21 *crooked*: Malignant.

25 *rehearse*: Repeat.

28 *Without false vantage*: In an equal match, fairly.

31 *held me glad of such a doom*: Considered myself lucky to be given such a sentence (instead of the death penalty).

32 *Have you the tongues*: Can you speak foreign languages?

33 *travel*: F has *trauaile* which was used interchangeably with 'travel' for both meanings. Therefore, although, strictly speaking, there is some doubt whether Valentine is attributing his linguistic skill to 'travel' or 'travail' (that is, work or study) in his youth, the latter seems unlikely in the context.

  happy: Facile, proficient.

35 *fat friar*: Friar Tuck of the Robin Hood legend.

36 *were*: Would be.

41–2 *anything to take to*: Any means of subsistence.

46 *awful*: Law-abiding, commanding respect. There is some plausibility in the suggestion that the compositor simply misread 'lawful', as there is no apparent reason for this particular word. However, the writing is such wretched stuff that it is useless to attempt to justify any word on literary grounds.

48 *practising*: Plotting, scheming.

49 *An heir, and near allied unto the Duke*: F's *And heire, and Neece, alide vnto the Duke* is usually emended in this way, on the grounds that the compositor probably misread 'neece' for 'neere', which was a common error and one which may have occurred in reverse in *King John*, II.1.424.

heir: This could be used of both sexes.

51 *mood*: Fit of anger.

58 *quality*: Profession, vocation.

60 *the rest*: Any other reason.

62 *To make a virtue of necessity*: A common proverb.

64 *consort*: Band, fellowship; accented on the second syllable.

69 *brag*: Report.

72 *silly*: Simple, thus 'helpless' or 'harmless'.
poor passengers: Travellers without money.

74 *crews*: Groups of confederates. It has been suggested that this is a misprint for 'caves' on the grounds that this would be more appropriate in view of line 75 and that a reference is made to a cave at V.3.12.

76 *dispose*: Disposal.

IV.2

This scene would appear at first sight to follow on directly from III.2 in which Thurio announces his intention of serenading Silvia. However, it is clear from Proteus's opening speech that some days have elapsed in which he has made use of the Duke's permission to visit his daughter.

3 *colour*: Pretence.

4 *prefer*: Urge, recommend.

5 *holy*: Good, virtuous. See the echo of this in the song at 40.

8 *twits*: Blames.

9 *commend*: Deliver, offer.

12–15 *And notwithstanding all her sudden quips . . . her still*: In *La Diana* it is noted of Felix (Proteus), 'the more he perceived that his lady forgot him, the more was his mind troubled with greater cares and grief which made him lead the most sorrowful life' (*Elizabethan Love Stories*, p. 151).

12 *sudden quips*: Sharp taunts or sarcastic utterances.

14 *spaniel-like*: Fawningly.

18 *crept*: Note the appropriateness of this word, which implies slyness, in connection with Proteus's character and behaviour.

19–20 *love* | *Will creep in service where it cannot go*: A common proverb.

20 *go*: Walk, as opposed to *creep*.

25–81 *Let's tune, and to it lustily awhile . . . Farewell*: This whole musical incident is quite closely paralleled in *La Diana*:

> The great joy that I felt in hearing him cannot be imagined; for methought I heard him now as in that happy and past time of our loves. But after the deceit of this imagination was discovered, seeing with mine eyes and hearing with mine ears that this music was bestowed upon another and not on me, God knows what a bitter death it was unto my soul! And with a grievous sigh that carried almost my life away with it, I asked mine host if he knew what the lady was for whose sake the music was made. He answered me that he could not imagine on whom it was bestowed, because in that street dwelled many noble and fair ladies. (*Elizabethan Love Stories*, pp. 138–9)

25 *Host of the Inn*: This character also figures largely in *La Diana*. The disguised Felismena (Julia) relates: 'Twenty days I was in going thither, at the end of which, being come to the desired place, I took up mine inn in a street least frequented with concourse of people' (*Elizabethan Love Stories*, p. 137).

26 *allycholly*: This mistake for 'melancholy' was perhaps a common one among the lower classes, as Mistress Quickly makes the same one in *The Merry Wives of Windsor*, I.4.148.

34–68 *The Musicians play*: Cf. *La Diana*:

> They began to wind three cornets and a sackbut with such skill and sweetness that it seemed celestial music. And then began a voice to sing, the sweetest, in my opinion, that ever I heard. And though I was in suspense by hearing Fabius speak, whereby a thousand doubts and imaginations, repugnant to my rest, occurred in my mind, yet I neglected not to hear what was sung, because their operations were not of

such force that they were able to hinder the desire nor
distemper the delight that I conceived by hearing it.
(*Elizabethan Love Stories*, p. 137)

37 *Song*: The whole serenade comprises (1) an instru-
mental introduction, (2) the song itself, (3) an instru-
mental postlude. Proteus presumably performs the solo
part. The song is justly one of the most popular
Shakespeare wrote. There is no extant contemporary
setting. It has been set to music by over fifty different
composers, including Thomas Arne, Edward German,
Roger Quilter, Eric Coates and Edmund Rubbra. The
best, and best-known, setting, of course, is Schubert's.

39 *swains*: Young men.

44 *For beauty lives with kindness*: Beauty flourishes in the
doing of generous actions.

45 *repair*: Hasten.

47 *inhabits*: Dwells.

53–68 *How now . . . but one thing*: The quibbling here is on
the correspondence, used by Shakespeare throughout
his career, between musical harmony (seen as the
earthly reflection of the harmony of the spheres) and
spiritual harmony in either the individual or the state
or the natural world. For a discussion of the dramatic
importance of this passage, see Introduction, pp. xviii, lii.

54 *likes*: Pleases.

55 *the musician likes me not*: Julia, meaning 'the musician
does not love me', quibbles on the Host's use of the
word *likes* at 54.

57 *plays false*: 'Is unfaithful' and 'plays a wrong musical
note'.

61 *a quick ear*: The Host still thinks that, because Julia has
detected a wrong note in the serenade, she is musically
discriminating.

62 *I would I were deaf*: Julia quibbles on the Host's word
quick taking it to mean an 'alive' as opposed to a 'dead'
or 'deaf' ear.
   slow: Heavy, dull. The meaning 'slow-beating' is
opposed to *quick*.

65 *Not a whit*: Not at all.

   jars: Grates.

66 *change*: A technical term used to describe a variation
   or modulation in musical compositions.

67 *change*: Change of affections.

   spite: Injury.

69 *I would always have one play but one thing*: Julia means
   that she would have only Proteus as her lover. There
   is a bawdy overtone in the phrase as Shakespeare often
   used the word 'play' as a metaphor for a man's making
   love to a woman.

70–73 *But, host, doth this Sir Proteus, that we talk on . . . all
   nick*: Cf. *La Diana*: 'To inquire of him of mine host I
   durst not, lest my coming might, perhaps, have been
   discovered' (*Elizabethan Love Stories*, p. 137). Felismena
   (Julia) is informed of Felix's (Proteus's) passion by his
   page.

70 *talk on*: Talk of.

73 *out of all nick*: Beyond all reckoning. The allusion is to
   the practice of keeping accounts or tallies by making
   'nicks' or notches on a stick. It is thus an appropriate
   phrase to be found in an innkeeper's mouth, or, considering Launce's lines at II.5.3–6, equally typical of him.

75–7 *Gone to seek his dog, which . . . he must carry for a present
   to his lady*: Launce does in fact present his dog to his
   master's lady (see IV.4.1–37), but it is not, as the Host
   says, *by his master's command* (see IV.4.43–57).

78 *parts*: Departs.

80 *drift*: Scheme, intention.

81 *Saint Gregory's Well*: There is, in fact, a well of this
   name near Milan.

   at an upstairs window: There is no general agreement
   among theatre historians as to the exact nature of the
   upper acting area of the Elizabethan stages. It would
   appear here that an open window rather than a balcony
   is all that is required.

89 *will*: Wish, desire.

   compass yours: Gain your good will. Proteus's quibble
   is on the meaning 'perform your least wish'.

90–101 *You have your wish; my will is even this . . . talking to*
       thee: In *La Diana*, Celia (Silvia) sends Felix (Proteus)
       a letter:

> For well thou mightest have denied, or not declared, thy past
> love, without giving me occasion to condemn thee by thine
> own confession. Thou sayest I was the cause that made thee
> forget thy former love. Comfort thyself; for there shall not
> want another to make thee forget thy second. (*Elizabethan*
> *Love Stories*, p. 145)

  91 *presently*: Immediately.
  92 *subtle*: Crafty.
  93 *conceitless*: Witless, lacking understanding.
  94 *To be*: As to be.
  97 *pale queen of night*: The moon. The reference is to
     Diana, who was also the goddess of chastity, and thus
     an appropriate figure for Silvia to swear by in her
     present situation.
 103 *'Twere false, if I should speak it*: It would be false even
     if Julia should say who has the right to claim it in two
     possible senses: (1) that Julia is 'dead' now that she is
     Sebastian; (2) that Julia might claim to have been 'killed'
     by Proteus's unfaithfulness.
 108 *importunacy*: Accented on the third syllable.
 114 *sepulchre*: Accented on the second syllable.
 115 *He heard not that*: He will deliberately ignore that.
 116 *obdurate*: Accented on the second syllable.
 118 *The picture that is hanging in your chamber*: There
     appears to be some connection between this reference
     and Proteus's words at II.4.207, to which see note.
120–22 *For since the substance of your perfect self . . . true love*:
       Contrast this with Valentine's diametrically opposite
       view on the same topic at III.1.174–7.
 120 *perfect*: Complete.
 121 *else*: Elsewhere, to another person.
     shadow: Lifeless person.
 122 *shadow*: Image, portrait.
 124 *shadow*: The quibble is on 'a lifeless person' and 'a

version of my true self' (as she is in disguise).

125 *your idol*: Contrast Proteus's denial of Silvia's capacity
to inspire worship when it is claimed for her by
Valentine at II.4.142–5.

126 *since your falsehood shall become you well*: Since it shall
be most appropriate to your falsehood.

127 *To worship shadows and adore false shapes*: The allusion
is to Proteus's name as well as to his nature. See headnote to I.1.

132 *By my halidom*: The word *halidom* was used to describe
anything regarded as sacred.

133–6 *Pray you, where lies . . . most heaviest*: Cf. *La Diana*:

> About dawning of the day the music ended; and I did what
> I could to espy out my Don Felix. But the darkness of the
> night was mine enemy therein. And seeing now that they
> were gone, I went to bed again, where I bewailed my great
> mishap, knowing that he whom most of all I loved had so
> unworthily forgotten me; whereof his music was too mani-
> fest a witness. (*Elizabethan Love Stories*, p. 140)

133 *lies*: Lodges.

134 *house*: Inn.

136 *watched*: Remained awake through.
most heaviest: Most depressing. The double superlative
is common in Shakespeare's grammar.

IV.3

Some editors make this scene merely a continuation of
IV.2. However, the scene is the day following and the
stage is obviously intended to be cleared before the
entrance of Eglamour.

8 *impose*: Command imposed.

9 *thus early*: Therefore, not much later than the time
when Julia and the Host left Silvia's window, when it
was *almost day* (IV.2.134).

13 *Valiant, wise, remorseful, well-accomplished*: The metre
is defective and there have been various suggestions
made for correcting it (see the second list of collations).

remorseful: Pitiful, compassionate.

14 *dear*: Affectionate.

16 *enforce me marry*: Force me to marry.

17 *Vain*: Empty, stupid.

abhors: F's *abhor'd* would appear to be a compositor's error, although it has been defended as a reference by Silvia to the time before she loved Valentine.

22 *I would to*: I wish to go to.

24 *for*: Because.

26 *repose*: Rely.

27 *Urge not*: Do not bring forward as an excuse (for not doing what I wish).

30–31 *a most unholy match . . . rewards with plagues*: Note the religious vocabulary used here in connection with love, as it is elsewhere in the play.

31 *rewards*: The singular verb form with two singular subjects is common in Shakespeare's grammar.

37 *grievances*: This word is usually glossed here as 'distresses, injuries' which in view of the following line appears to me to be impossible. Dr Johnson's suggestion 'sorrowful affections' which are *virtuously . . . placed* with Valentine is far more likely. The word is used in this sense also at III.2.86.

40 *Recking*: Caring.

betideth: Befalls.

41 *befortune*: Befall, betide.

44 *confession*: Pronounced with four syllables here.

IV.4

It is obvious from 83 that, as in IV.3, the scene is before Silvia's tower. However, Eglamour departs at dawn, whereas Launce enters after dinner (i.e. after noon). From this it has been suggested that a scene has been omitted between IV.3 and IV.4.

2 *of*: From.

4 *to it*: To drowning, to death.

4–6 *I have taught him, even as one would say precisely, 'Thus I would teach a dog.'*: I follow F's punctuation; for the suggested alternative reading see the second list of collations.

8 *steps me*: The expletive *me* indicates that an interest in the proceedings was felt by the person indicated. See also the same usage at 16 and 23.

9 *trencher*: Wooden plate.

capon's: Chicken's.

10 *keep himself*: Restrain himself, exercise self-control.

12 *a dog at*: Adept at.

13–14 *to take a fault upon me*: To take the blame for the fault myself.

18 *bless the mark*: This phrase was used parenthetically as an apology when something unacceptable was being said. Originally it was a formula for averting evil omens.

a pissing while: A colloquial term meaning 'a very short time'. However, Launce also means it literally: 'the duration of time necessary for Crab to urinate'.

23 *the fellow that whips the dogs*: The kennel man.

26 *wot*: Know.

29 *stocks*: A common punishment for acts of theft.

puddings: A savoury dish made of stuffed animal intestines.

31 *pillory*: In the pillory the prisoner was fastened by the head and hands, as opposed to the stocks in which he was fastened by the legs.

34 *Madam Silvia*: It is possible that this should be 'Madam Julia', considering that Launce, in the incident as he describes it, would have had little opportunity for 'taking leave' of Silvia. Also Launce is asking Crab to remember, which suggests that he is referring to a previous incident.

39 *presently*: Straight away.

41 *whoreson*: A coarse pleasantry.

45 *jewel*: F has this word capitalized which may suggest that the dog's name is indicated. This is a possibility, although the capitalization practice of F does not merit such confidence.

47 *currish*: Ignoble, mean-spirited. The pun is with *cur* at 46.

52 *squirrel*: An indication of the size of the dog, but the

word has also been taken to be the name of the dog.

53 *hangman boys*: F has *Hangman's boyes*; but the meaning is almost certainly 'boys fit for the hangman, rough-necks'.

54–5 *a dog as big as ten of yours*: Despite this line, in theatrical productions the dogs range from a small wretched animal to something resembling the Hound of the Baskervilles.

59 *still an end*: Continuously, perpetually.
    turns me to shame: Brings shame upon me.

60–86 *Sebastian, I have entertainèd thee . . . and solitary*: In *La Diana* Felismena (Julia) tells how she was employed by Felix (Proteus):

Don Felix, as soon as he was come forth . . . commanded me the same night to come to him at his lodging. Thither I went, and he entertained me for his page, making the most of me in the world; where, being but a few days with him, I saw the messages, letters, and gifts that were brought and carried on both sides – grievous wounds, alas! and corsives to my dying heart . . . But after one month was past, Don Felix began to like so well of me that he disclosed his whole love unto me, from the beginning unto the present estate and forwardness that it was then in, committing the charge thereof to my secrecy and help, telling me that he was favoured of her at the beginning, and that afterwards she waxed weary of her loving and accustomed entertainment, the cause whereof was a secret report (whosoever it was that buzzed it into her ears) of the love that he did bear to a lady in his own country . . . 'And there is no doubt,' said Don Felix unto me, 'but that indeed, I did once commence that love that she lays to my charge. But God knows if now there be anything in the world that I love and esteem more dear and precious than her.' When I heard him say so, you may imagine . . . what a mortal dagger pierced my wounded heart. But with dissembling the matter the best I could, I answered him thus: 'It were better, sir, methinks, that the gentlewoman should complain with cause, and that it were so indeed. For if the other lady, whom you served before, did not deserve to be

forgotten of you, you do her (under correction, my lord) the
greatest wrong in the world.' 'The love,' said Don Felix again,
'which I bear to my Celia will not let me understand it so.
But I have done her, methinks, the greatest injury, having
placed my love first in another, and not in her.' 'Of these
wrongs,' said I to myself, 'I know who bears the worst away.'
(*Elizabethan Love Stories*, pp. 144–5)

60–69 *Sebastian, I have entertainèd thee ... Silvia*: Cf. Orsino's
lines to Viola in *Twelfth Night* (I.4.24–36):

> O, then unfold the passion of my love.
> Surprise her with discourse of my dear faith.
> It shall become thee well to act my woes;
> She will attend it better in thy youth
> Than in a nuncio's of more grave aspect ...
> For they shall yet belie thy happy years
> That say thou art a man. Diana's lip
> Is not more smooth and rubious ...
> I know thy constellation is right apt
> For this affair.

Orsino also sends Olivia a jewel by Viola.

60 *entertainèd*: Taken into service.

64–6 *But chiefly for thy face and thy behaviour ... truth*: It is
ironical that Proteus should (1) so readily recognize
these qualities in the face of his mistress, and (2) prize
them so highly in view of his own behaviour.

65 *augury*: Prophetic skill.

68 *presently*: Immediately.

70 *well delivered*: Well (who) delivered.

71 *to leave*: To part with.

72 *belike*: In all likelihood.

73–81 *Alas! ... cry 'Alas!'*: Cf *La Diana*:

> 'If thy grief doth suffer any counsel,' said I, 'that thy thoughts
> be divided into this second passion, since there is so much
> due to the first.' Don Felix answered me again, sighing, and
> knocking me gently on the shoulder, saying: 'How wise art

thou, Valerius, and what good counsel dost thou give me –
if I could follow it!' . . . 'I think, sir, it is needless to amend
this letter, or to make the gentlewoman amends to whom it
is sent, but her whom you do injury so much with it.'
(*Elizabethan Love Stories*, pp. 146–7)

82 *therewithal*: With it.

83 *That's her chamber*: There has been a great deal of
discussion about the location of this scene, many editors
pointing out that there is an imaginary change of place
from outside to inside the tower after Proteus's exit,
which is necessary because Silvia is a prisoner in the
tower. Other editors have seen the difficulty as resulting
from abridgement of the text. See An Account of the
Text.

90 *poor fool*: Referring to herself.

96–9 *And now am I, unhappy messenger . . . dispraised*: Cf.
Viola's speech in *Twelfth Night* (I.4.40–42): 'I'll do my
best | To woo your lady. (*Aside*) Yet, a barful strife! |
Whoe'er I woo, myself would be his wife.'

96–7 *And now am I, unhappy messenger, | To plead for that
which I would not obtain*: Cf. Felismena's similar lament
in *La Diana*: '"O thrice unfortunate Felismena, that
with thine own weapons art constrained to wound thy
ever-dying heart, and to heap up favours for him who
made so small account of thine"' (*Elizabethan Love
Stories*, pp. 150–51).

98, 99 *would have*: Desire to have.

100–104 *I am my master's true confirmèd love . . . him speed*: Cf.
Viola's words in *Twelfth Night* (II.2.33–8):

> My master loves her dearly;
> And I, poor monster, fond as much on him . . .
> My state is desperate for my master's love.
> As I am a woman – now, alas the day . . . !

104 *speed*: Succeed, prosper.

105 *mean*: Agent, means.

106 *where to speak*: Where I may speak.

115–17 *Tell him from me . . . this shadow*: Silvia's attitude on
the value of the image as opposed to the reality of the
loved one is similar to Valentine's at III.1.174–84.

117 *shadow*: Image, portrait. Silvia probably also implies
the meaning 'mere nothing'.

119 *unadvised*: Inadvertently.

120 *Julia takes back the letter she offers and gives Silvia another
one*: There seems little point in Julia first offering by
mistake what is obviously one of Proteus's letters to
herself and then handing Silvia the right one, unless
in a fuller version of the play the idea was more
completely developed.

127 *new-found*: Recently invented.

137 *tender*: Have a tender regard for.

139–69 *Dost thou know her . . . very sorrow*: Cf. *La Diana*:

'Dost thou then know Felismena,' said Celia, 'the lady whom
thy master did once love and serve in his own country?' 'I
know her,' said I, 'although not so well as it was needful for
me to have prevented so many mishaps' – and this I spake
softly to myself – 'for my father's house was near to hers.'
. . . Celia began in good earnest to ask me what manner of
woman Felismena was; whom I answered that, touching her
beauty, some thought her to be very fair; but I was never of
that opinion, because she hath many days since wanted the
chiefest thing that is requisite for it. 'What is that?' said Celia.
'Content of mind,' said I, 'because perfect beauty can never
be where the same is not adjoined to it.' (*Elizabethan Love
Stories*, p. 149)

140–69 *Almost as well as I do know myself . . . very sorrow*: Julia's
description of herself and Silvia's unawareness of the
device is similar to that in which Viola describes her
own love for Orsino under the guise of talking about
her sister in *Twelfth Night* (II.4.106–8): 'My father had
a daughter loved a man – | As it might be perhaps,
were I a woman, | I should your lordship.'

142 *several*: Different.

143 *Belike*: In all likelihood.

150 *sun-expelling mask*: As the standard of feminine beauty in Elizabethan England was fair, the more fashionable and courtly women of the time protected their complexions against sunburn by means of masks or, more commonly, stiffened velvet headpieces called 'bongraces'.

152 *lily-tincture*: White colour.

153 *That*: So that.
    black: Dark-skinned (from sunburn).

155–69 *About my stature . . . very sorrow*: For comment on these lines, see Introduction, pp. xliii–xliv.

155–6 *at Pentecost, | When all our pageants of delight were played*: Whitsuntide had long been associated with public celebrations in England. The religious mystery cycle plays had been performed at this time of the year in some parts of the country, as were May games, and (according to *The Winter's Tale*, IV.4.134) 'Whitsun pastorals'.

156 *pageants of delight*: Pleasant performances.

157 *the woman's part*: All female roles were played by boys on the Elizabethan stage.

158 *trimmed*: Dressed.

162 *agood*: In earnest.

164–5 *'twas Ariadne passioning | For Theseus' perjury and unjust flight*: Ariadne was the daughter of Minos, king of Crete. She fell in love with Theseus, prince of Sparta, and, after helping him slay the Minotaur, fled with him, only to be abandoned by him on the Isle of Naxos.

164 *passioning*: Sorrowing, passionately grieving.

166 *lively*: Adverbial.

170 *beholding*: Indebted.

178 *cold*: Ineffectual, coldly received.

182 *tire*: A term applied to women's headdress generally, although Julia appears to be referring to the type of headwear that set off the face, such as the French hood or the reticulated caul or coif.

186 *auburn*: Whitish, flaxen.
    perfect yellow: The natural colour of Queen Elizabeth

I's hair and, consequently, a fashionable colour.

188 *a coloured periwig*: False hair was extensively used by Elizabethan women.

189 *grey*: Used to describe blue eyes.

190 *as high*: A high forehead was much admired as an aspect of female beauty.

192 *But I can*: That I cannot.

respective: Worthy of respect, likely to inspire respect.

193 *fond*: Foolishly doting.

194 *shadow*: Julia can be considered such because of her disguise and because her treatment by Proteus has made her a 'lifeless version' of her former self.

take . . . up: The quibble is on 'pick up' and 'oppose, accept the challenge'.

this shadow: The portrait of Silvia. See notes to IV.2.121, 122, 124.

195 *senseless*: Insensible.

197 *sense*: Rational meaning.

198 *statue*: Julia is setting herself as a substantial image against the *shadow* – the two-dimensional image of the painting.

199 *use*: Treat.

V.1

6 *expedition*: Haste; pronounced with five syllables.

9 *postern*: Small side door.

12 *recover*: Reach.

sure: Safe, secure.

V.2

1–29 *what says Silvia to my suit . . . by lease*: The same device for poking fun at a fool is in *Cymbeline*, I.2 and II.1.

3 *takes exceptions at*: Makes objections to, finds fault with.

5 *too little*: Proteus's allusion is perhaps to Thurio's excessively thin legs.

6 *boot*: Riding-boot.

7 *JULIA*: F assigns this line to Proteus and 13–14 to Thurio. However, in view of the design of the scene, they are almost certainly comments by Julia on the conversation between the two men.

spurred: The quibble is with *boot* (meaning 'riding-boot') at 6.

9 *a fair one*: Pale or fresh-complexioned. The suggestion is thus one of effeminacy.

10 *black*: Swarthy.

12 *Black men*: Dark-complexioned men.

13 *pearls*: Julia quibbles on the proverb by taking the word *pearls* in its medical sense: 'cataracts'.

14 *wink*: Shut my eyes.

16 *Ill, when you talk of war*: This also carries the suggestion of effeminacy.

20 *makes no doubt of that*: Does not question it, since Silvia, like Julia, has perceived its true quality.

23 *derived*: Descended, well born.

24 *from a gentleman to a fool*: Julia quibbles on 'descended', the understood meaning of *derived*.

26 *pities them*: Proteus is probably quibbling on the two meanings of *possessions*: 'property' (which Silvia despises) and 'possessions by evil spirits' (which Silvia pities).

28 *owe*: Own, possess.

29 *out by lease*: Let to others (thus not under his own control). It has been suggested that Proteus is alluding to Thurio's mental endowments.

35 *peasant*: Base person.

40 *masked*: See note to IV.4.150.

44 *discourse*: Accented on the second syllable here.

45 *presently*: Immediately, post-haste.

46 *mountain-foot*: Foothills.

49 *peevish*: Foolish, perverse, wayward.

V.3

4 *learned*: Taught.
   brook: Endure.

6 *gentleman*: Sir Eglamour.

8 *Moyses*: This was a common Elizabethan form of the name Moses.
   Valerius: This is the name under which Felismena in *La Diana* goes when disguised as her lover's page.

14 *will not use a woman lawlessly*: See IV.1.71–2.

V.4

1–3 *How use doth breed a habit in a man . . . towns*: Cf. the exiled Duke's speech in *As You Like It* (II.1.2–3): 'Hath not old custom made this life more sweet | Than that of painted pomp?'

1 *use*: Custom.
  habit: Settled practice, custom, usage.

2 *shadowy desert*: Deserted place shaded by trees. Some editors take *desert* to be adjectival; see the second list of collations.

3 *brook*: Endure, but closer to 'like' in the context.

5 *nightingale's complaining notes*: The allusion is to the classical myth that Tereus raped Philomela who was turned into a nightingale which sang with its breast pressed against a thorn when Tereus's mistreatment was remembered.

6 *record*: Sing like a bird.

7 *inhabit*: Lodge.

9 *growing ruinous*: Brought to ruin.

12 *cherish*: Treat with kindness.
  forlorn: Accented on the first syllable.
  swain: The word is being used here in the pastoral sense of 'lover' rather than 'rustic'.

15 *Have*: Who have.

19 *this service*: Rescued her from the outlaws.

20 *respect*: Regard, heed.

21 *him*: Silvia was accompanied by the First Outlaw when Proteus rescued her, the Second and Third Outlaws having gone in pursuit of Sir Eglamour; see V.3.9–14.

23 *meed*: Reward.

24 *boon*: Gift.

31 *approach*: Amorous advance.

37 *tender*: Precious, dear.

43 *still approved*: Continually confirmed by experience.

47–9 *thou didst then rend thy faith . . . perjury*: The idea in these lines is quite clear although exception has often been taken to the strained metaphor in the passage. For the various suggested emendations, see the second list of collations.

49 *to love me*: In loving me.

53–4 *In love,* | *Who respects friend*: Cf. *Much Ado About Nothing* (II.1.160–61): 'Friendship is constant in all other things | Save in the office and affairs of love . . .'

54 *respects*: Takes into account. The conflict between love and friendship was a feature of Romance literature and had its most famous Elizabethan expression in John Lyly's *Euphues, The Anatomy of Wit* (1578).

57 *at arms' end*: At sword's point.

61 *fashion*: Kind, sort.

62 *common*: As opposed to 'unusual', but also carrying the meaning 'base'.

67 *Who should be trusted now, when one's right hand*: F's reading *Who should be trusted, when ones right hand* is clearly defective in a passage of regular blank verse, and so I have adopted the emendation from F2. For other suggestions see the second list of collations.

73 *confounds*: Ruins. The singular verb form with two singular subjects is common in Shakespeare's grammar.

76 *tender*: Offer.

77 *commit*: Sin, transgress.

78 *receive*: Acknowledge.

83 *All that was mine in Silvia I give thee*: See An Account of the Text. In Thomas Elyot's *The Book named the Governor*, which has been suggested as a possible source for the play, Gisippus tells his friend Titus: 'Here I renounce to you clearly all my title and interest that I now have or might have in that fair maiden' (p. 216).

86 *wag*: Boy.

88–96 *O, good sir, my master . . . to Silvia*: Because this passage contradicts the action at IV.4.129–34, and as Silvia is inexplicably silent, many critics have suspected abridgement at this point; see An Account of the Text.

95 *cry you mercy*: Beg your pardon.

98 *depart*: Departure.

102–10 *Behold her that gave aim to all thy oaths . . . their minds*: In *La Diana*, Felix (Proteus) and Felismena (Julia) have a final meeting in which Felismena strikes a similar note: '"In the habit of a tender and dainty lady I loved

thee more than thou canst imagine; and in the habit of
a base page I served thee (a thing more contrary to my
rest and reputation than I mean now to rehearse)''
(*Elizabethan Love Stories*, p. 156).

102 *gave aim to*: Was the object of.

104 *root*: Bottom of the heart. The allusion is to the stud
marking the centre of an archery target (continuing
the metaphor started by Julia at 102).

105 *this habit*: Her page's clothes.

106 *took*: Taken.

107–8 *if shame live | In a disguise of love*: If there be anything
shameful in a disguise assumed because of love. It is
possible that Julia is alluding to Proteus's duplicity: 'if
there is any shame in someone who is but a false repre-
sentation of the lover'.

111–16 *Than men their minds . . . constant eye*: In *La Diana*,
Felix (Proteus) undergoes a similar rapid repentance:
'When the knight heard Felismena's words, and knew
them all to be as true as he was disloyal, his heart by
this strange and sudden accident recovered some force
again to see what great injury he had done her'
(*Elizabethan Love Stories*, p. 156).

112 *constant*: Faithful, loyal.

114 *Inconstancy falls off ere it begins*: The inconstant man is
unfaithful before he even begins to love.

115–16 *What is in Silvia's face . . . constant eye*: In *La Diana*
much is made of the superiority of Felismena's (Julia's)
beauty to Celia's (Silvia's).

118 *close*: Union, with perhaps an allusion to the musical
meaning 'a harmonious ending after discord'.

127 *give back*: Retire, back off.

128 *measure*: The reach (of a sword).

130 *Verona shall not hold thee*: This is the last of the
geographical confusions in the play. Thurio is, of
course, a citizen of Milan. See An Account of the Text
and the second list of collations.

hold thee: Keep you safe. The emendation 'hold me'
has been suggested with some plausibility.

132 *I dare thee but to breathe upon my love*: This strikes a

different note from Valentine's lines offering Silvia to
Proteus, and perhaps provides some support for the
suggestion of deliberate ambiguity in the line; see note
to 83.

138 *make such means*: Make such efforts, take such pains.

139 *such slight conditions*: Such easy terms; *conditions* has
     four syllables here.

142 *worthy of an empress' love*: Cf. II.4.74, where the Duke
     describes Proteus in the same terms. Some editors have
     taken this to mean that Silvia is the Duke's heir.

144 *repeal*: Recall.

145 *Plead a new state*: The term is from rhetoric, with *state*
     meaning 'the point in question or debate between
     contending parties, as it emerges from their pleadings'.
     The Duke is saying that he takes up a new position (on
     the question of Valentine's merits).

147 *derived*: Descended.

153 *kept withal*: Lived with.

157 *They are reformèd, civil, full of good*: This is presum-
     ably the result of Valentine's restraining influence, but
     is hardly consistent with what we have heard at 14–15.

161 *include*: Conclude.
     jars: Discords, disagreements.

162 *triumphs*: Pageants, public festivities.
     solemnity: Festivity.

163 *dare be bold*: Will presume.

166–7 *I think the boy hath grace in him . . . more grace than
       boy*: The Duke's allusion is to the proverb 'Blushing is
       virtue's colour' (bashfulness is a sign of grace).
       Valentine quibbles on the other meaning of *grace*, 'a
       graceful woman'.

170 *That*: So that.
     wonder: Marvel at.
     fortunèd: Happened.

172 *discoverèd*: Disclosed.

173 *our*: Valentine's and Silvia's.

The National: three theatres and so much more…

www.nationaltheatre.org.uk

In its three theatres on London's South Bank, the National presents an eclectic mix of new plays and classics, with seven or eight shows in repertory at any one time.

And there's more. Step inside and enjoy free exhibitions, backstage tours, talks and readings, a great theatre bookshop and plenty of places to eat and drink.

Sign-up as an e-member at www.nationaltheatre.org.uk/join and we'll keep you up-to-date with everything that's going on.

NATIONAL THEATRE
SOUTH BANK
LONDON SE1 9PX

PENGUIN SHAKESPEARE

MEASURE FOR MEASURE
WILLIAM SHAKESPEARE

WWW.PENGUINSHAKESPEARE.COM

In the Duke's absence from Vienna, his strict deputy Angelo revives an ancient law forbidding sex outside marriage. The young Claudio, whose fiancée is pregnant, is condemned to death by the law. His sister Isabella, soon to become a nun, pleads with Lord Angelo for her brother's life. But her purity so excites Angelo that he offers her a monstrous bargain – he will save Claudio if Isabella will visit him that night.

This book includes a general introduction to Shakespeare's life and the Elizabethan theatre, a separate introduction to *Measure for Measure*, a chronology of his works, suggestions for further reading, an essay discussing performance options on both stage and screen by Nicholas Arnold, and a commentary.

Edited by J. M. Nosworthy

With an introduction by Julia Briggs

General Editor: Stanley Wells

PENGUIN SHAKESPEARE

THE MERCHANT OF VENICE
WILLIAM SHAKESPEARE

WWW.PENGUINSHAKESPEARE.COM

A noble but impoverished Venetian asks a friend, Antonio, for a loan to impress an heiress. His friend agrees, but is forced to borrow the sum from a cynical Jewish moneylender, Shylock, and signs a chilling contract to honour the debt with a pound of his own flesh. A complex and controversial comedy, *The Merchant of Venice* explores prejudice and the true nature of justice.

This book includes a general introduction to Shakespeare's life and the Elizabethan theatre, a separate introduction to *The Merchant of Venice*, a chronology of his works, suggestions for further reading, an essay discussing performance options on both stage and screen, and a commentary.

Edited by W. Moelwyn Merchant

With an introduction by Peter Holland

General Editor: Stanley Wells

PENGUIN SHAKESPEARE

A MIDSUMMER NIGHT'S DREAM
WILLIAM SHAKESPEARE

WWW.PENGUINSHAKESPEARE.COM

A young woman flees Athens with her lover, only to be pursued by her would-be husband and by her best friend. Unwittingly, all four find themselves in an enchanted forest where fairies and sprites soon take an interest in human affairs, dispensing magical love potions and casting mischievous spells. In this dazzling comedy, confusion ends in harmony, as love is transformed, misplaced, and – ultimately – restored.

This book includes a general introduction to Shakespeare's life and the Elizabethan theatre, a separate introduction to *A Midsummer Night's Dream*, a chronology of his works, suggestions for further reading, an essay discussing performance options on both stage and screen, and a commentary.

Edited by Stanley Wells

With an introduction by Helen Hackett

General Editor: Stanley Wells

PENGUIN SHAKESPEARE

MUCH ADO ABOUT NOTHING
WILLIAM SHAKESPEARE

WWW.PENGUINSHAKESPEARE.COM

A vivacious woman and a high-spirited man both claim that they are determined never to marry. But when their friends trick them into believing that each harbours secret feelings for the other, they begin to question whether their witty banter and sharp-tongued repartee conceals something deeper. Schemes abound, misunderstandings proliferate and matches are eventually made in this sparkling and irresistible comedy.

This book includes a general introduction to Shakespeare's life and the Elizabethan theatre, a separate introduction to *Much Ado About Nothing*, a chronology of his works, suggestions for further reading, an essay discussing performance options on both stage and screen, and a commentary.

Edited by R. A. Foakes

With an introduction by Janette Dillon

General Editor: Stanley Wells

PENGUIN SHAKESPEARE

ROMEO AND JULIET
WILLIAM SHAKESPEARE

WWW.PENGUINSHAKESPEARE.COM

A young man and woman meet by chance and fall instantly in love. But their families are bitter enemies, and in order to be together the two lovers must be prepared to risk everything. Set in a city torn apart by feuds and gang warfare, *Romeo and Juliet* is a dazzling combination of passion and hatred, bawdy comedy and high tragedy.

This book includes a general introduction to Shakespeare's life and the Elizabethan theatre, a separate introduction to *Romeo and Juliet*, a chronology of his works, suggestions for further reading, an essay discussing performance options on both stage and screen, and a commentary.

Edited by T. J. B. Spencer

With an introduction by Adrian Poole

General Editor: Stanley Wells

PENGUIN SHAKESPEARE

TIMON OF ATHENS
WILLIAM SHAKESPEARE

WWW.PENGUINSHAKESPEARE.COM

After squandering his wealth with prodigal generosity, a rich Athenian gentleman finds himself deep in debt. Unshaken by the prospect of bankruptcy, he is certain that the friends he has helped so often will come to his aid. But when they learn his wealth is gone, he quickly finds that their promises fall away to nothing in this tragic exploration of power, greed, and loyalty betrayed.

This book includes a general introduction to Shakespeare's life and the Elizabethan theatre, a separate introduction to *Timon of Athens*, a chronology of his works, suggestions for further reading, an essay discussing performance options on both stage and screen, and a commentary.

Edited by G. R. Hibbard

With an introduction by Nicholas Walton

General Editor: Stanley Wells

PENGUIN SHAKESPEARE

TWELFTH NIGHT
WILLIAM SHAKESPEARE

WWW.PENGUINSHAKESPEARE.COM

Separated from her twin brother Sebastian after a shipwreck, Viola disguises herself as a boy to serve the Duke of Illyria. Wooing a countess on his behalf, she is stunned to find herself the object of his beloved's affections. With the arrival of Viola's brother, and a trick played upon the countess's steward, confusion reigns in this romantic comedy of mistaken identity.

This book includes a general introduction to Shakespeare's life and the Elizabethan theatre, a separate introduction to *Twelfth Night*, a chronology of his works, suggestions for further reading, an essay discussing performance options on both stage and screen, and a commentary.

Edited by M. M. Mahood

With an introduction by Michael Dobson

General Editor: Stanley Wells